# Prioritize 'til It Hurts

# Prioritize 'til It Hurts

*Discovering and Unleashing Your Best Opportunities*

By Rodolfo Salas

University Press, Inc.
2003

ISBN 0-9726982-0-5



First Edition Published
January 2003



2003 University Press, Inc.
Printed and Manufactured in
the United States of America
First Printing

# Contents

*In memory of Charlie Hugo –*
*An inspiration to all who knew him.*

# Acknowledgements

I must first acknowledge the support and encouragement of my immediate family who made it possible for me to achieve my vision. A special thank you to my wife, Bunny, and to my children for their unwavering confidence and encouragement throughout the process. Special thanks to my brothers and sisters, in particular Ricardo who has transformed, refined and enhanced my thinking onto highly interactive and user friendly Internet- based "thinking tools". And finally to my sister in law, Siobhan Onthank, who produced my beautiful presentation slides for free when I got started on my own.

---

I would also like to express my deep appreciation to those who created opportunities for me throughout my career. In their own unique ways they have all impacted my professional development and made me a wiser and a more effective professional: Art Anton, Kim Caldwell, Bill Cosgrove, Léon Danco, Don Davis, Rod Fallow, Dave Given, Preben Hadberg, Mike Kirchoff, "Whitey" Oberg, Tracey O'Rourke, Bill Redfield, Michael Salkind, Dean Scarborough, David Scheible, Sister Diana Stano, Don Stoebe, Earl Wheeler, Bob Williams, Tom Williams, and Mike Wojno.

---

And finally to my friends and associates who have unselfishly given their time and helped me clarify my own thinking. I am sure they will recognize many of our conversations in these pages: Geoff Baker, Rita Brauneck, Diane Connelly, Gary Ervick, Dave Hazard, Pradip Kamat, Larry Lederman, Dave Lowman, Bob Mason, Doug McIntosh, Tracy McNally, Deborah Mills-Scofield, Jim Nerpouni, Lee Nielsen, Charly Pelanne, Mike Salvador, Edward Siegel, Turk Smith, Joe Tirpak, Steve Tricamo, Dave Watterson, and Laverne Wilson. A special thank you to Tom Grill who told me several years ago: "If you want to excel at anything, prioritize until it hurts, then cut another 10%."

# Introduction

You are holding in your hands a book that teaches a proven System to explore and better understand your "unique universe." I will share with you ways to continuously discover opportunities, prioritize your options, and follow-through to achieve success.

Prioritization, the central theme of this book, is actually a liberating experience. Once we choose where we will focus, we can align our organizations around a common purpose to get the right things done.

Getting the right things done, however, requires thorough understanding of the options available to us, confidence to make the tough choices, and commitment to make it happen.

When I was a child, a neighbor asked me if I could help her clean her windows. She said to me, "Please make sure you get the corners really clean." I was puzzled. Did she want me to only clean the corners? But then she explained, "If you focus on cleaning the corners, you will find that the rest off the window is much easier to clean." She then shared with me that all good window cleaners know this.

Many organizations look back at their accomplishments to find they worked extremely hard on too many things. They created a lot of stress for themselves, and yet failed to achieve the level of performance required to move to the next level.

Our challenge as executives is to find the "corners", those few things we must do extremely well. And once we find them, we are able to create a platform for achieving excellence and can execute with much less effort.

**When we do a few right things extremely well, we cause many other things to improve.**

If the benefits are so great and so obvious, why do most of us find the process of prioritization so excruciating? Why does it hurt?

Is it because we are afraid to leave things off the list just in case one of them might hold the key to our success? Is it because it's so hard to discontinue a pet project even when our customers tell us they don't need or want it? Is it because we don't understand the opportunities, the issues and the implications of one option versus another? Or is it because we lack the courage and commitment to excellence and to making the tough choices.

**If we don't make the tough choices, we leave to chance where it is that we will excel, and in the end rarely achieve major success.**

*Figure A* – ***Integrated View***

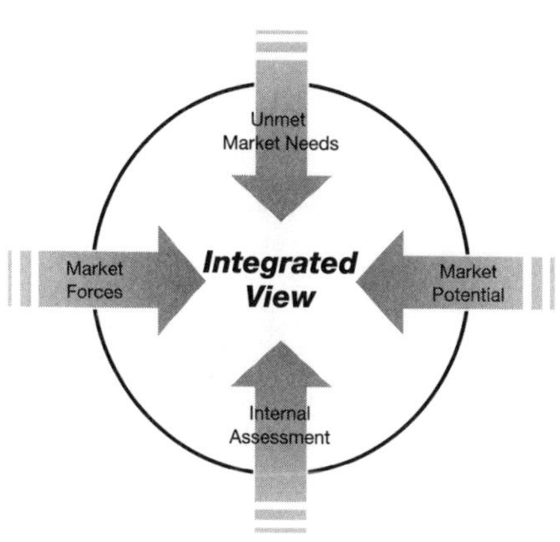


In the first five chapters of this book I will share simple but powerful "thinking tools" that fit together like a puzzle they enable you to develop an integrated view of your environment and *discover your best opportunities*.

In the final chapters I will share techniques that help you align your organization *and unleash these opportunities*.

One step at a time I will describe the cause-and-effect dynamics that are present in any environment, regardless of industry segment, organization size, or where in the world we live.

Understanding and applying these “rules’ enables us to continuously discover ways to:

- Target markets that offer us the greatest potential for profitable growth,
- Anticipate major opportunities and challenges in the marketplace,
- Create unique value for our customers,
- Establish a clear identifiable difference,
- Optimize performance across the value chain,
- Build competencies for long-term advantage,
- Raise barriers to competition,
- Change the rules of play in the marketplace, and…

…Achieve a sustainable competitive advantage.

The “Prioritize ‘til it Hurts” System has enabled me to help thousands of executives reduce complexity and align their organizations to get the right things done.

This book is my effort to “prioritize til it hurts”. In it I want to communicate what I believe are the essential elements for creating clear market differentiation and sustainable profitable growth.

I hope the book will stimulate your thinking, increase your confidence to make the tough choices, and help you to enhance and fine-tune your roadmap for success.

# ***Prioritize 'til It Hurts***

*Discovering and Unleashing Your Best Opportunities*

By Rodolfo Salas

University Press, Inc.
2003

# 1

## Understanding Our "Unique Universe"

Why do organizations get themselves into trouble even when they have excellent resources and a well-earned reputation?

Many organizations operate with a limited view of the possibilities that surround them. Perhaps because they have failed to take an *integrated view* of their own "unique universe," or have become too comfortable with what they see, hear and feel around them.

It's like a family that has lived in the same place for many years and observes its neighborhood through the same familiar living room window day in and day out. But no one seems to notice that the neighborhood and their home have deteriorated over time and no longer appeal to a prospective buyer. The changes have been so gradual and imperceptible that there seems to be little need or motivation to want to change it or improve it.

We just need to look around to see the many changes that continue to have an impact on our business and our organization. Any view through the same familiar "window" will, at a minimum, be limited in scope. More importantly, with the rapid pace of change occurring today, chances are our organization may be looking at the "neighborhood" through the wrong "window."

**The good news is that all organizations operate within an integrated system with predictable and consistent cause-and-effect dynamics.**

Understanding these cause-and-effect dynamics not only helps us to anticipate and prevent trouble before it occurs, but it enables us to put the right pieces in place and take our organization to a higher level.

This book describes a system that helps us "take the roof off our building," gain an *integrated view* of our "unique universe," make our choices, and get moving to achieve new levels of success.

There are "Acres of Diamonds" out there for us to discover. In this book I will share tools to uncover and to go after them.

### *Acres of Diamonds*

*Acres of Diamonds* is a book by Russell H. Conwell from the 1960s. In it he tells of an old Persian, Ali Hafed, who owned a very large farm. Although he was a wealthy and contented man, one day, a Buddhist priest told him about the riches that he could accumulate if he set out to search for diamonds. The priest convinced him that he could find diamonds "along the rivers that run through the white sands, between high mountains." As Conwell tells the story, the farmer "had not lost

anything, but (now) he was poor because he was discontented, and discontented because he feared he was poor."
Upon realizing he could become immensely rich, he sold his farm, left his family with friends and set out to search for diamonds along the riverbanks.

After years of disappointment, he threw himself into the ocean and drowned.

After his death, the new owners of his old farm discovered in their property the largest diamond in the world. And after further investigation, they found more diamonds in this old property. Ironically, this old farmer had been living on the largest diamond field in the world and had abandoned it to look for diamonds elsewhere.

The moral of the story is this: We, as organizations and individuals, are sitting on "acres of diamonds" but simply can't see them. Like the farmer, we spend our time in the wrong places, wasting time and energy, rather than searching for diamonds which are probably under our own two feet.

This chapter is about searching for and finding the diamonds that will provide us sustained profitable growth into the future.

Examining and understanding our "unique universe" in search of "Diamonds" may appear daunting at first. However, the Strategic Scan® model described in this chapter enables us to make what may appear vast and overwhelming, seem logical and approachable.

*Figure 1 –* ***Strategic Scan®***

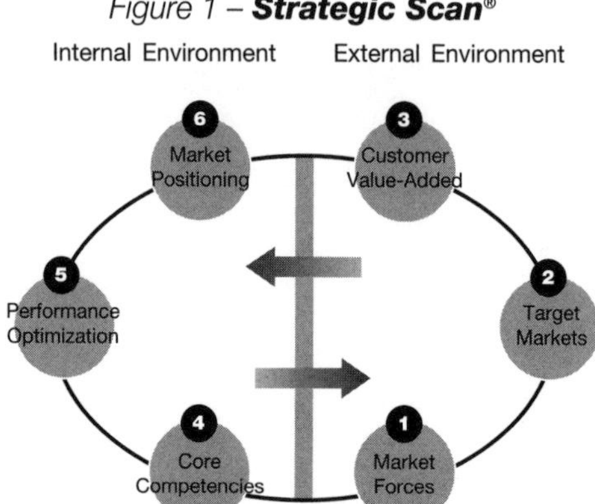


This initial and high-level representation of the Strategic Scan® *(Figure 1 – Strategic Scan®)* depicts the *broad* elements we need to pay attention to in our external environment on the right, and our internal environment on the left.

Our external environment is comprised of:

1 – Market forces,

2 – Our target markets, and

3 – Value our customers expect and demand from us,

Our internal environment is comprised of:

4 – Our core competencies,

5 – How we measure and optimize performance, and

6 – How we position ourselves to win in the marketplace.

Once we understand our universe and the dynamics within it, we need to prioritize, focus and remain focused to make things happen.

*Figure 2 –* ***Strategic Scan®***

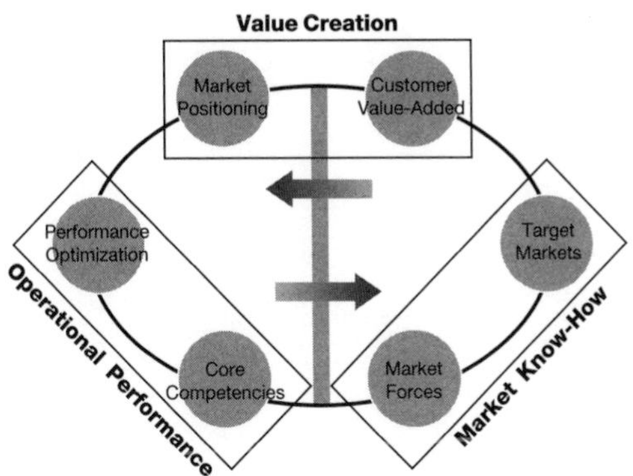


To further simplify the Strategic Scan,® I have grouped the "bubbles" into three "boxes."

The ***Operational Performance*** box represents our internal management priorities. The ***Market Know-how*** box represents our target markets and the forces that surround them. The ***Value Creation*** box is our formula or template for making a difference to our customers and for achieving major impact in our marketplace.

Getting the right things done for the customer and having the customer recognize our contributions will lead to a clear and positive identifiable difference in the marketplace *(Figure 2 – Strategic Scan®)*.

---

**Our key indicator for success and our reward will be sustained revenue and profit growth. This is how our customers' tell us that we have exceeded their expectations and that they appreciate what we do for them.**

---

*Figure 3* – ***Strategic Scan®***

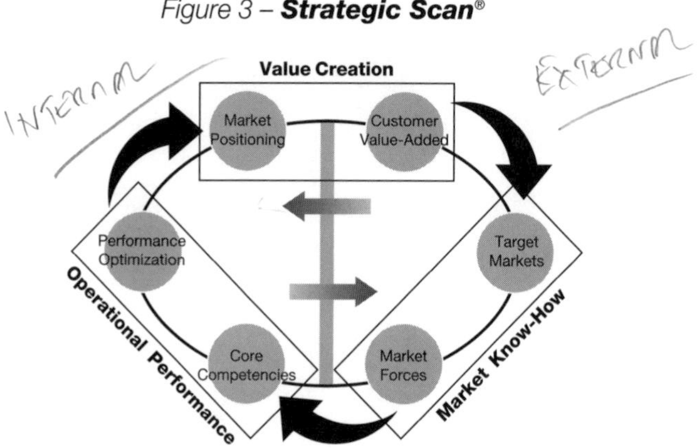


When a corporation is up and running, the flow of organizational activities is predominantly clockwise *(Figure 3 – Strategic Scan®)*. Our customers express their needs and place their orders (across the bottom of the model), we position ourselves, and deliver products and solutions to satisfy their needs (across the top). And as long as we continually exceed customer expectations and maximize our profit growth potential, our business model works.

*Figure 4 –* ***Strategic Scan®***

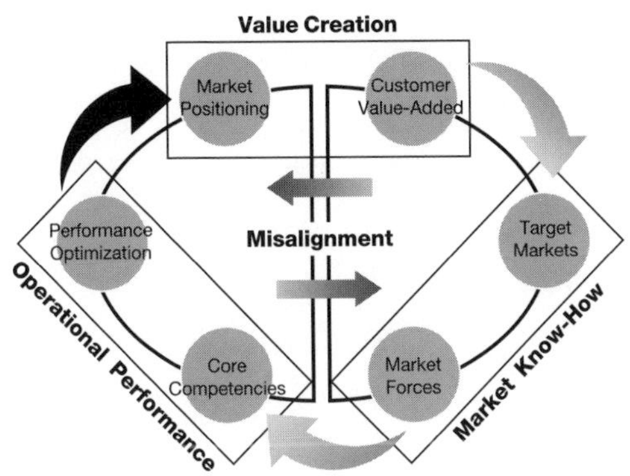


Often, what happens over time is that the two-halves of our "unique universe" come apart *(Figure 4 – Strategic Scan®)*. It happens because we are drawn to solve internal problems… people problems, supplier problems, money problems, and perhaps we take our position for granted. We are forced to spend more time on our company internally and less and less time listening to our customers and creating value for them (note the faded arrows).

As this happens, our products and services become less and less relevant to the markets we serve, and even though we seem to be working just as hard, what reaches the customer is not necessarily what the customer is looking for. We have become misaligned with the marketplace. Our selling model no longer matches our customers' buying model.

It seems to be a natural progression: When we start a new venture we are very close to our customers, but over time, regardless of the reasons, we become more and more distant and less and less relevant.

When we get caught up in this internal "box" we spend our days going from meeting to meeting. The symptoms are classic: meetings become lengthier, we don't seem to reach conclusions on critical issues, we constantly run behind schedule, internal mail seems to grow exponentially, and at times we feel that we are getting nowhere.

Chances are that the problems we are experiencing are but mere symptoms of a larger and more serious problem. To solve the underlying problem, we need to realign our thinking and our organization with the priorities of the marketplace.

The Strategic Scan® model forces that discipline by *reversing* the way we look at our "unique universe." We start by focusing and dedicating more time and effort to understanding the markets we want to serve *(Figure 5 – Strategic Scan®)*.

Once we truly understand the needs and the dynamics of our target markets (Market Know-how), we will better understand our opportunity space. We will know how to position ourselves for success, to create value, to exceed market expectations, and become a dominant player.

*Figure 5 –* ***Strategic Scan®***

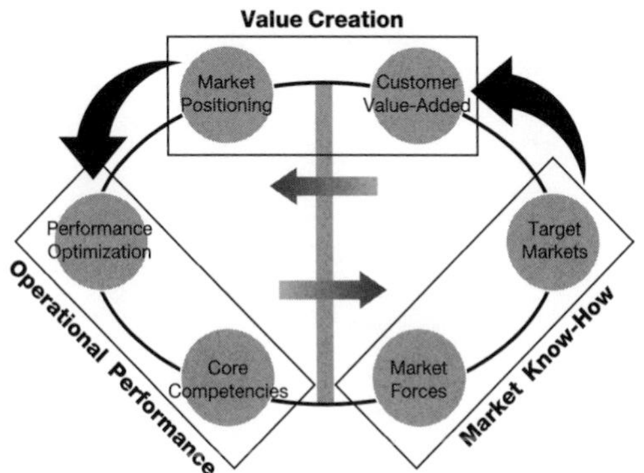


With this value-creation template in hand, we can now determine what we must do to align our organization with the marketplace, re-invent ourselves if necessary and drive operational performance improvements.

We are now in a position to strike a balance between *building* our organization to recreate the entrepreneurial spirit that made us successful in the first place, and *managing* our business to maintain a solid financial footing.

Once we align our organization, we can run our business in a normal "clockwise" direction with confidence that we will reach much higher levels of performance.

# 2

## *Visualizing Our Journey of Discovery*

Just as the Strategic Scan® helps us understand our "unique universe" by viewing it in a counter-clockwise direction *(Figure 6 – Strategic Scan®)*, the "Baseball Diamond" *(Figure 7 – Running the Bases)*, will serve as our *roadmap* for exploring that universe and uncovering our own "Acres of Diamonds."

Regardless of whether we understand the game of baseball or not, we will find this "four-point diamond" can help us visualize, understand and stay on track throughout our *journey*. The linkage between the two models, and all that we need to know about the game of baseball, will become evident in this brief introductory chapter.

### *"Running the Bases"*

In the next three chapters I will demonstrate that by "running the bases" in sequence, we can uncover many possibilities while building an *integrated view* of our business.

To realize the full potential of the System, however, we need to engage our organization in the process. Only then will we have a team that is aligned, equipped to make the right choices, and committed to getting the right things done.

*Figure 6* – ***Strategic Scan®***

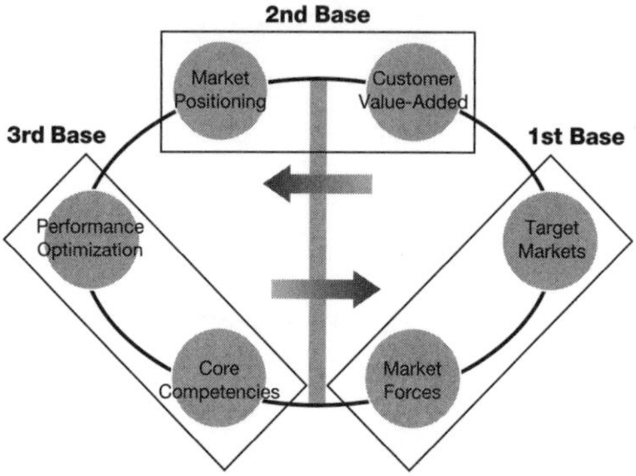

2nd Base
Market Positioning
Customer Value-Added
3rd Base
1st Base
Performance Optimization
Target Markets
Core Competencies
Market Forces

*Figure 7* – ***Running the Bases***

To be Our Customers' #1 Choice
2
3
1
H
To be Our Competitors' Worst Nightmare
To Discover Our Opportunity Space
To Achieve Organizational Effectiveness

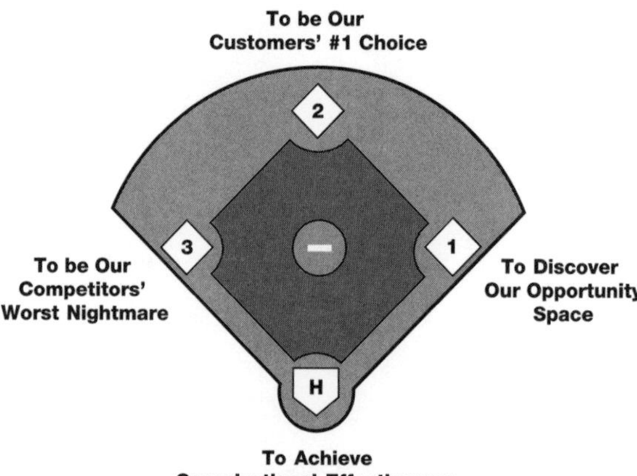

"1st base" will be our first stop. Our objective will be to better *understand* where we have the *best opportunities*, determine how to align our organization with the market, and create our critical path for profit. It is here that we will build our initial model for success. One that we can later test and validate as we complete a full 360° review of our business or endeavor. This is the most important step of the process.

Then, and only after we have built our model for success, should we move to "2nd base." Here we will discuss strategies for understanding the dynamics of our targeted markets, for capturing the unmet needs of our targeted customers and for creating our own identifiable difference.

Having decided where we want to focus ("1st Base"), and having a solid understanding of market dynamics and customer unmet needs ("2nd Base"), we will be ready to target specific competitors at "3rd Base" and discuss strategies for becoming their worst nightmare.

By the time we round "3rd base," and prior to moving to "Home Plate," we will have an *integrated view* of our environment and we will *understand* the many options available to us. We will know the actions that we must take internally and externally to achieve our goals.

At Home Plate we will then have the elements to prioritize our options, implement a winning plan and *unleash our best opportunities (Please see Chapters 6 - 9).*

Often some of us are inclined to run the bases backwards. See if you recognize the pattern:

Typically we will start at "first base" and set our financial targets. Then, instead of running the "bases" in sequence to discover *our best opportunities,* we go straight "home" to *unleash* the obvious ones. For example we may decide to outsource certain products or services, reorganize the company, re-deploy resources, or even make one or two acquisitions.

Next we proceed to "3rd Base" to implement our competitive strategies. Unfortunately, we often do it without really understanding the market dynamics. Then at "2nd base," we visit our customers, not to understand their unmet needs, but to sell them our products and services. And finally we return to "1st Base" to measure performance vs. plan and determine corrective actions.

In a fast changing environment, this process can produce lots of work and disappointing results.

When we allow this behavior pattern to persist, usually we will find ourselves working very hard while struggling to keep up with day-to-day activities.

If we are caught in this dilemma, chances are that we have become misaligned with the marketplace and are spending too much time putting out fires that should have been anticipated or prevented. Consider running the bases in sequence.

Under the direction of a qualified facilitator or coach, it should only take a few days of your personal time to develop an *integrated view* of your business or endeavor. You will then be pleased to see how easy and logical it becomes to prioritize and make the right choices.

In the next chapter we will begin our journey to discover our "acres of diamonds." But before we begin our journey we need to establish our destination.

## *Establishing Stretch Goals*

If we are to build and maintain a vibrant, competitive organization we need to periodically bring ourselves to that thin line between what is possible and what is impossible.

We will need to establish "stretch goals"" at the beginning of the planning process. We should never scale back prematurely. We owe it to ourselves to step out of our comfort zone from time to time and discover creative ideas to achieve what may at first appear "impossible."

You might ask: "Why don't we wait until we complete the planning process and have a much better understanding of the opportunities and constraints that lie before us? Wouldn't we come up with better, more accurate stretch goals then?"

There are many real life examples to refute this premise, but here is only one: Imagine if John F. Kennedy had decided to challenge his nation to "put a man on the moon and bring him back alive this decade," only *after* the astronauts were trained, rockets were built and all the detail planning was completed. Chances are it would have never happened.

By establishing a vision and committing to getting it done, the project unified and exhilarated the nation. It spawned unanticipated programs that have resulted in numerous breakthroughs in medicine, electronics, materials, and photography to name just a few.

Stretch goals, properly set, will cause us to reach out for things we consider far-fetched, but nevertheless exciting and truly worthwhile. Stretch goals will get us to "step out of the box," they will help us uncover new possibilities, and they will drive us to craft innovative strategies that can position us to win consistently.

Stretch goals can actually help us break down departmental barriers and get everyone energized and focused toward a unified purpose.

Once we have an *integrated view* of our business or endeavor, and we are prepared to set our final priorities, we should adjust our goals (if necessary) to assure they are achievable, affordable and consistent with our overall vision and core values.

# 3

## *Discovering Our Opportunity Space*

At "1st base" we will begin our journey by determining our opportunity space *(Figure 8 – Strategic Scan®; Figure 9 – Running the Bases)*. That is, where we must focus in the market place to drive top line and bottom line growth. Initially this step will help us determine which geographic sectors, industry segments, applications, channels of distribution, and products and services will provide us that opportunity. Then, it will help us to determine the actions we must take internally to actually make it happen.

Here are several examples that illustrate the benefits of this exercise:

### Example #1

The first is about a company that had evolved to become a multi-divisional organization without an overall strategic plan. Each division was independent with its own general manager, its own sales and marketing organization, and its own overhead structure. Their prospects for major growth were minimal and their overhead structure was large, duplicative and costly.

*Figure 8* – ***Strategic Scan®***

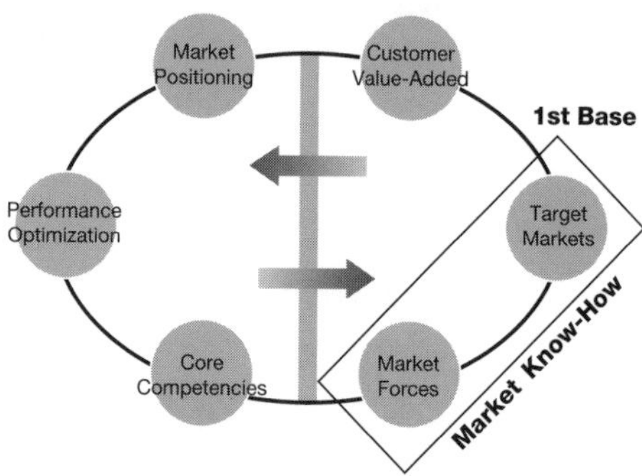


*Figure 9* – ***Running the Bases***

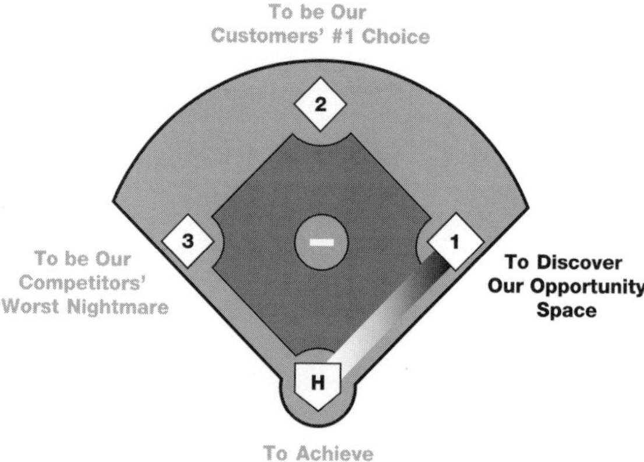

In an attempt to look at their business strategically, management first set out to understand the total business. They wanted to know where there may exist synergies among the divisions, where there may be major opportunities for profit growth, and where they lacked critical capabilities. They also wanted to know if parts of their business didn't fit within an overall plan for growth.

The "1st Base" exercise enabled division heads and the corporate staff to visualize the various options available to them. Once they understood the ideal combination of technologies, products, channels of distribution and markets to drive sustainable growth; they were able to come together on how to restructure the company.

They chose to build two highly synergistic groups by consolidating six of the nine divisions. Each of these two groups would now focus on complementary technology areas, delivering integrated solutions to well understood and clearly targeted markets.

The three remaining divisions were sold and the resulting capital was used to acquire other small companies that complemented the two newly created groups.

This experience did not require rocket science, but it represented a major discovery that required prioritization and alignment of all the critical functions of the business, and resulted in economies of scale and a doubling of revenues and profits in two years.

**Example #2:**

The second is about a company whose sales were declining due to competitive pressures. They decided to use the "1st Base" exercise to determine where they needed to focus to generate short-term profitable growth. The "1st Base" exercise made it clear to the company CEO and to the functional heads that the greatest potential for short-term growth was not from expansion into new geographic markets, nor from new product offerings, nor from new uses of their products. Instead, their *best opportunity* was to further penetrate their key accounts.

Their sales force was unfocused and sold to accounts of all sizes. The situation had evolved over the years and not a lot of attention had been paid to it. As a result of their discovery, they developed an effective top to bottom program to penetrate these key accounts. This included major penetration targets by account, full support from headquarters, and assignment of top people in the company to the project. The following year they grew their top line by 15%.

**Example #3**

This is about a mid-sized manufacturing organization that had experienced losses for three consecutive years. At first it was difficult to understand why this was happening and what it was they could do about it.

After several iterations on "1st base" they discovered the problem.

Eager to gain significant orders, they were continuously lured into battle against their two major competitors. Both competitors were low cost producers prepared to drop prices to win these significant orders. In the end, the smaller company competed on price, sometimes won these significant orders, but always lost money on the deals.

Why was this happening? Why was it difficult for them to see what was happening to them?

First their sales force was paid and motivated to deliver top line revenue rather than profit. Any single order represented a huge portion of their annual quota so that's where they focused their attention. Second, their promotional efforts were directed at attracting major consumers of their products. They paid little attention to smaller consumers. Third, their production facilities and their service structure were optimized to respond to significant orders. They were unable to respond efficiently to smaller lot sizes. Fourth, they did not know their true costs and had little basis for establishing responsible pricing. They never really knew if they were making or losing money on any given order.

The organization had succeeded in aligning its thinking, its resources and its organizational structure to support what the sales force was selling. And this was about to put them out of business.

By analyzing the various combinations of customer types and sizes, and the many potential uses for their products and services, they were able to discover a niche market where their major competitors had little incentive to compete. This was their best opportunity to establish a dominant position and drive profitable growth.

To secure this new opportunity space, they redesigned and refocused their marketing and promotional efforts, redirected and retrained their sales force, changed sales incentives, changed their distribution channels, recalibrated their production facilities, and streamlined their processes to better understand and take cost out of the business.

The discovery enabled them to deliver an 11% profit within 18 months.

**Example #4**

This is about a premier electronics firm that was supplying engineering design components to end-users but was lagging far behind the overall growth of the industry. However, they did not understand why this was happening.

At "1st base" they discovered that most of the revenue and profit growth was taking place downstream in their own value chain. Smaller systems integrators were packaging components from original manufacturers like them, and delivering "plug-and-play" solutions to the end users. End users no longer wanted to buy components from original manufacturers and preferred instead to buy integrated solutions that were ready for use.

The electronics firm had a major challenge: they had no expertise building or delivering fully operational solutions to end-users. They needed to transform themselves from a components manufacturer to a systems integrator if they wanted to compete in this market. This required a major strategic shift and a change in culture.

Rather than attempting this feat from within the organization, they chose to create a separate independent business that would nurture a new and different culture, attract and develop new skills, establish new and innovative business practices, leverage their technologies wherever possible, partner with complementary suppliers to build integrated solutions, and expand their channels of distribution to sell and service these complete solutions.

It was a major undertaking no doubt but the results were dramatic: They grew revenues and profits by five-fold in four years.

I can cite example after example but as you can see, "1st Base" is all about finding our "Acres of Diamonds." That is, finding where we have the basic capabilities to be the best and make a profit doing it. Success then follows by prioritizing 'til it hurts and getting everyone aligned and pulling in the same direction to get it done.

It is not until we focus on a few areas where we know that we can be the best, and where we want to be the best, that we can produce these types of dramatic results.

To get there is difficult, it's hard, and it takes time to analyze the situation. It usually requires several passes "over the target" to understand the different options.

Our search for "diamonds" starts by examining every possible way for generating revenues and profits. We need to take the time to sit back and look at all of the opportunities before us, objectively, using common sense. Assume that we are starting with a blank canvas, like an artist who is trying to produce a new and fresh painting devoid of pre-conceived notions.

*Figure 10 –* ***Critical Path for Profit***

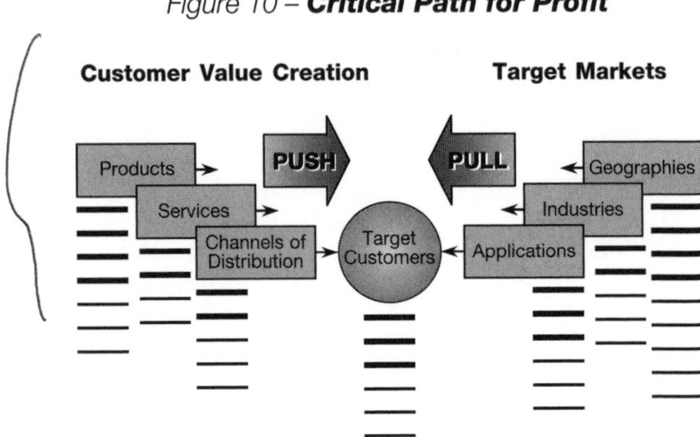


Then we can hone in on those few areas where we can be the best, align everyone along our value chain to achieve excellence, take action and reap the benefits that are sure to come.

---

**Sometimes the best ideas are hidden. When searching for major opportunities or facing critical situations, we need to take the time to uncover every possibility before coming up with our final short list.**

---

We start by identifying *(Figure 10 – Critical Path for Profit)*, from left to right, current and future products, technologies or services that we can offer, and every channel of distribution that we could utilize. Then we identify every potential customer by type such as key accounts, Other Equipment Manufacturers (OEMs), Regional Accounts. Finally, from right to left, we identify every geographic sector, industry segment, and application where our products and services can be put to use and where we can create demand.

This is an iterative process that requires several passes before we can be sure that we have drawn a complete view of our business or endeavor.

Once we complete this phase of the process we have a powerful tool that helps us analyze all of our options objectively and expands our *opportunity space*.

Look for ways to maximize and balance the "push" and "pull" forces along the value chain. In other words, which products, customers, applications, etc. give us the best opportunity to excel and achieve market dominance. We need to trust our instincts; we know more than we might at first think.

The final step is to prioritize elements in each column to create our "critical path for profit."

---

**When we do a few things extremely well,
we cause many other things to improve.**

---

For example, if we deliver exceptional performance in a particular product, the improvements that we make in skills, processes, and technologies, may benefit other products, customers and applications.

Most companies keep track of sales and profits by product, channels of distribution, customer types, industry segments and geographic segments. However, very rarely do they track sales or profits by application.

Yet it is in the *application* of our products and services, in the use of these, where we will find “acres of diamonds.” It is here, at the point of use, that users perceive value, and it is here that we have an opportunity to differentiate ourselves.

For example, if we manufacture general-purpose containers, it is likely that we don’t track the percentage of sales or profits by the particular use of our containers (e.g.: storage, insulation or transportation). My experience, however, is that even though we may not be tracking sales and profits by applications, we do have a pretty good idea as to what our products are being used for, where our customers have the greatest demand, and where we have the greatest opportunity to differentiate ourselves to drive profit growth.

Step out of your comfort zone and determine where you really need to focus. Don’t be afraid to prioritize ‘til it hurts to reach your stretch goals. Direct your resources, internally and externally, to excel where you can differentiate yourself. Discontinue or de-emphasize applications that no longer can contribute to your profitable growth. And remember this:

---

**Unless we prioritize, we may work very hard,**
**but never excel at anything.**

---

# 4

## *Becoming Our Customers' #1 Choice*

At "2nd base" we will continue on our journey *(Figure 11 – Strategic Scan®; Figure 12 – Running the Bases)*. Here we want to know how we can exceed our customers' expectations and create our own identifiable difference. But until we have determined at "1st base" where we must deliver exceptional performance to drive profit growth, we won't know for sure who our customer will be. Technically we won't have a "man on base" ready to run to "2nd base."

Once we do have a "man on base" and have reached "2nd base," our challenge is to get our team comfortable talking and listening to those customers in those markets where we need and want to be clearly differentiated. For example: customers who have been loyal to us, those who have gone to competitors, those who are upset with us, and those with whom we have not yet made contact.

This step is so critical, that if our organization cannot effectively complete it, we should strongly consider having an expert do it for us.

*Figure 11* – ***Strategic Scan***®

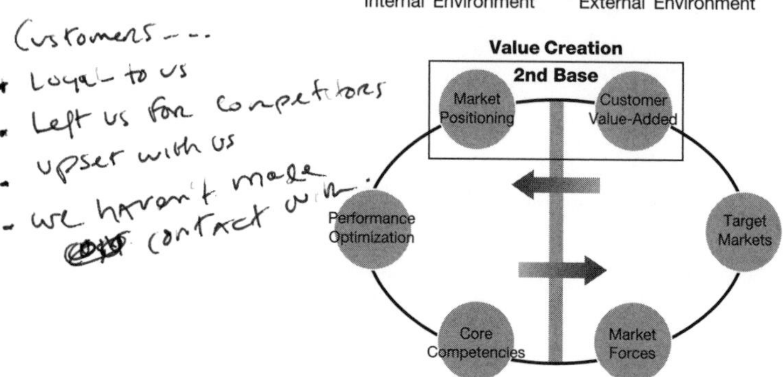


*Figure 12* – ***Running the Bases***

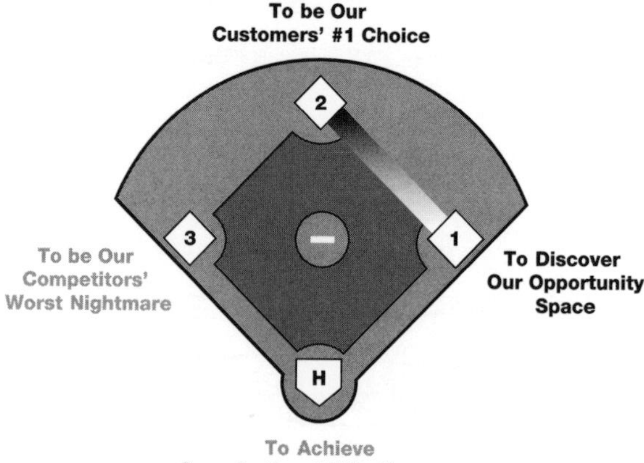

I recall many instances where an executive has said to me, "what we sell is such an insignificant portion of our client's total expense that their decision makers don't want to talk to us." I encourage them to just go do it. I say, "talk with them like no other vendor ever talked with them. Ask them about what is important to them; ask them about the things that concern them, the things that keep them awake at night." And they say, "Oh, they won't talk to us about those things." And I say, "Trust me, just go and try it."

In nine out of ten situations we deal with reasonable customers, people who have aspirations, people who have real problems, people who may not have anyone else with whom to share their thoughts; and just the fact that we express concern and interest about them, about where they are trying to take their business, and what may be getting in their way, makes a huge difference.

Executives I have worked with, invariably get back to me and say, "you know, once my customer started talking, s/he just kept on talking, sharing more and more about their dreams and their concerns, and that led to talking about ways that we could help them." And guess what… these executives just found a new friend in their customer, and their customers just found a new friend in them. Their customers found someone who was interested in listening to them, someone who wanted to dialog with them, someone who sincerely wanted to help. And that can turn out to be nearly miraculous.

Not wanting to approach our key customers is acting like the young man who is afraid to ask the beautiful girl for a date on Saturday night because he is certain that she already has a date. But in reality the beautiful girl spends most Saturdays alone because no one asks her out. There are many clients out there who are like that beautiful girl. We may not want to approach our key customers because we are afraid they don't have the time, or they don't want to be bothered by us. And when we approach them, we find that they are delighted to talk with us.

And when we talk with them, we find ways that we can help them, and this is what it's all about. "2nd base" is about *discovering* unmet needs and establishing close relationships that are built on empathy and trust.

When we accomplish this we become much more of a *partner* to our customers and much less of a "widget" salesman.

Therefore, we need to interview key players in selected industries and in selected geographies and try to learn as much as we can from our customers and prospects. We must discover *how* we can earn their trust and *how* we can become their *supplier* of choice.

As we conduct these "voice of the customer" interviews, we need to refrain from telling them too much about what we already have to offer. First, listen to understand how they feel: Get inside their "heads," their "guts" and their "hearts." Listen to understand their concerns and their dreams. Discover innovative solutions that will satisfy unmet needs and exceed their expectations.

Learn to talk with our customers both as their *partner* and as their *supplier* to capture the total picture *(Figure 13 – Partner Relationship)*. There are cause-and-effect dynamics here that are crucial to uncovering opportunities. Allow me to explain:

*Partners* never start meetings discussing pricing or delivery schedules. Instead they share their dreams, their vision of where they are trying to take their business or endeavor: Where they feel pain and can use help.

Together they and we will determine if, where and how they need help to achieve their goals or to reduce their costs and improve profitability. We need to use these opportunities to strengthen our relationship.

---

***Partners* stay together when they work together to improve revenues (make money), lower costs (save money), and enjoy and strengthen their relationship (feel good).**

---

- When partners discuss a business expansion opportunity or requirement, "growing revenues and profits" will probably be their main topic of conversation.
- When they discuss a price-sensitive or cost-sensitive situation, then "lowering costs" is likely to be their main topic for discussion.
- Otherwise, they will probably talk about things that make them feel good about each other: their families and friends, playing the next round of golf, or other personal matters.

*Figure 13* – ***Partner Relationship***

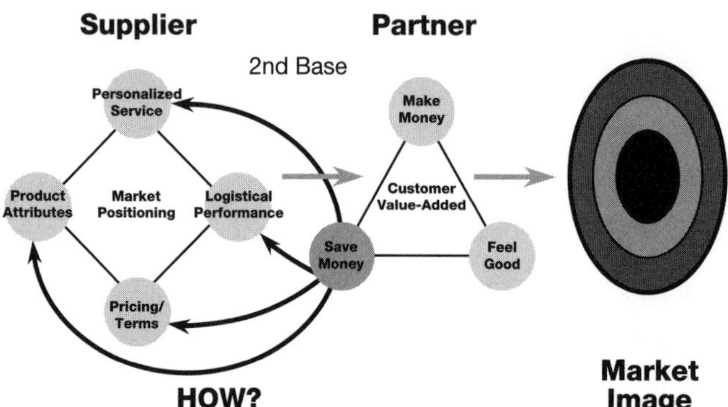


Once we understand what our customers are yearning for and what they really want to accomplish (as *partners*), then we will be better positioned to determine *how* we can make a real difference for them as their *supplier*.

---

**If we want to become and remain our customers' preferred supplier, we must perform or excel along four dimensions: personalized services, product and service attributes, logistical performance, and terms & conditions (including price).**

---

For example, if we learn that one of our key customers has a serious inventory cost problem, we can as their *supplier*, look for unique ways to help them solve this problem. Perhaps we can provide them personalized services from an inventory control expert, or implement a focused quality program to reduce defective components, or offer consignment inventory, or implement a Just-in-Time delivery program for them.

If we want to be our customers' preferred *supplier*, we must understand how we can best create value for them as a *supplier*. That is:

- "How can we differentiate ourselves through *personalized services* such as on-site support, personal training, or advice and counsel? Doctors, lawyers, consultants, travel agents, and architects differentiate themselves especially along this dimension.

- How can we differentiate ourselves through *product and service attributes* such as quality, functionality, appearance, responsiveness, or ease of use? Manufacturers of automobiles, computer projectors, industrial machines, and sports equipment primarily differentiate themselves here.

- How can we differentiate ourselves through *logistical performance* such as delivering what our customers order, where they want it, how they want it, and when we promised it. The postal service, catalog houses and express mail companies pay special attention to this dimension of value creation.

- How can we (or do we want to) differentiate ourselves through *terms and conditions* such as bargain pricing, payment terms, and other conditions of doing business? Discount stores and commodity sellers differentiate themselves here.

We must listen, and listen hard, to what our customers are demanding from their suppliers. If we are to be their *supplier* of choice, we need to be competitive on all four dimensions described above. In addition, we need to achieve exceptional performance in at least one of these dimensions. Doing so, will create a positive market image, build our brand, and produce our identifiable difference ("ID") in the marketplace.

If we think of any organization (or personality) that has achieved a positive "ID" in the marketplace, we are likely to describe their "ID" along one of these four dimensions:

1 – Personalized Services
2 – Product Attributes
3 – Delivery Performance, or
4 – Pricing and Terms.

As we align our organization, remember this:

---

**If we are excellent at items 1, 2 and 3, we will position ourselves to justify higher pricing and gain higher margins. However, if we are deficient in any of these three dimensions, we will be forced to cut internal costs, compete on price, and possibly suffer the consequences with lower margins.**

---

Figure 14 – **Supplier Relationship**

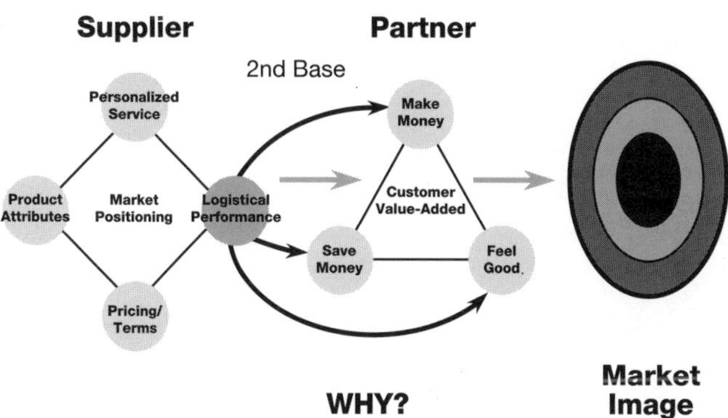


When our discussions with our customers focus primarily on *supplier* issues, we need to ask them "*why*" they are demanding these things. This is how we learn directly from them the real business issues and opportunities. By simply taking this step we can move the conversation from that of a *supplier* to that of a *partner (Figure 14 – Supplier Relationship).*

Once we are successful in making this shift we will build stronger, lasting partnerships. We will gain a better appreciation of how we can help our customers succeed in their business, and where we need to focus to achieve our own stretch goals.

---

**"Connecting the dots" between what our customers tell us they need to achieve *their success* (as partners), and what we need to do to help them achieve *their success* (as their supplier), is crucial to aligning our organization to achieve *our own success.***

---

If we limit our discussions with our customers to *supplier* type discussions, we will risk having to respond to their demands rather than helping them solve their business problems.

Remember that our "unique universe" is comprised of predictable cause-and-effect dynamics. Take advantage of these dynamics to understand your customers' unmet needs, make a positive difference for them by being both a good *partner* and a good *supplier*.

### *External Forces*

We don't live in a static environment. Changes will occur in our marketplace. Our customers' needs and expectations will change based on new challenges and opportunities that they will face, and on new options that we and our competitors provide to them. While we cannot anticipate exactly everything that will happen, we can position ourselves to respond to most any eventuality by developing the proper competencies in specific areas of our business.

We must take the time to understand industry trends, competition, and technology breakthroughs as we go "around the bases." Particularly, we need to study those trends that can have a major positive or negative impact on us and/or our customers.

A single event has the potential for changing the rules of play in our marketplace. For example: a technological innovation, a new law, or the unexpected merger of two competitors.

---

**Organizational misalignment always begins with a change in the marketplace that went unnoticed by us.**

---

Remember how the invention of the semiconductor in the late 60s transformed the entire computer industry and changed our lives in so many ways. Consider the impact of graphite as it transformed tennis, skiing and other sports. Finally, think about the impact that anti-pollution legislation has had on many industries such as steel and automotive.

Consider using the "***S.W.O.T***. *Analysis*" technique to analyze variables in your environment and to choose the best path for your business.

**S.W.O.T.** enables us to summarize and prioritize *today's* **S**trengths and **W**eaknesses (or pluses and minuses) of a particular technology, competitor, or of any situation, and *tomorrow's* **O**pportunities, and **T**hreats for your business.

---

**There is always new news. If unfolding events catch us by surprise, we are likely to miss opportunities and suffer the consequences.**

---

# 5

## *Becoming Our Competitors' Worst Nightmare*

At "3rd Base" we will complete developing an *integrated view* of our "unique universe" *(Figure 17 – Strategic Scan®; Figure 18 – Running the Bases)*.

"3rd base" is about becoming our competitors' worst nightmare. But it makes no sense to go to "3rd base" until we have successfully gone through "1st Base" and "2nd Base."

Why? Because we first need to know *where* we will compete, *against whom* we must compete, and *how* we must compete to win.

I recall several instances where executives have completed their competitive assessment exercise at "3rd base" and said to me, "Do you see what we see?" And I asked, "What do you see?" and they said, "You know, we just discovered that we are pretty good at things our customers don't care about, and we are not so good at things they feel passionate about." These executives had just discovered how vulnerable they were in areas they were not paying attention to, and they had also discovered they were expending resources in areas that didn't matter as much to the customer.

*Figure 15 –* ***Strategic Scan®***

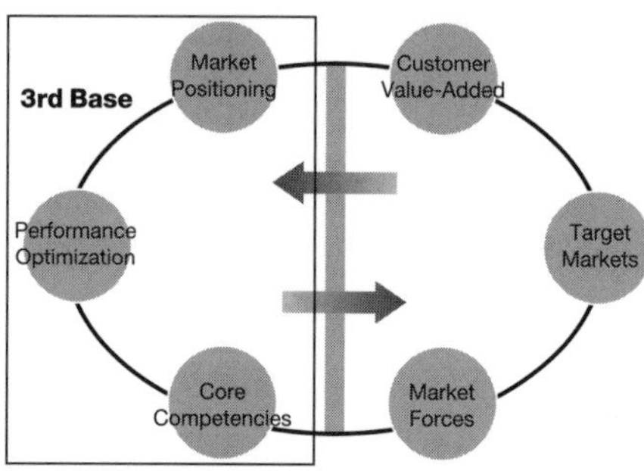


*Figure 16 –* ***Running the Bases***

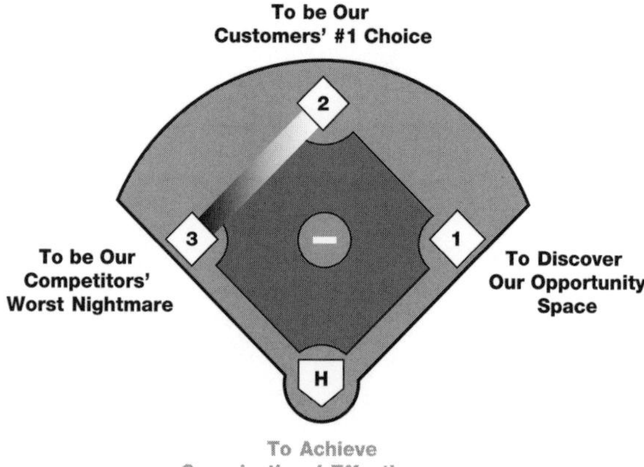

I remember working with a company that was very much internally focused and product driven. They spoke about product innovation and cost reductions as their top two priorities. Until they got to "3rd Base," they were quite comfortable with their priorities. It wasn't until they compared their analysis of customer needs with their own internal capabilities, and with their assessment of their competitors' capabilities, that they discovered their Achilles heel.

As important as product innovation and cost reductions were to their survival, they discovered at "3rd base" that their product delivery and service performance was not only unacceptable to their customers but a major weakness against competition.

Someone once told me, "There is nothing as motivating as shear panic!" Needless to say, this led to a realignment of priorities by this company.

In both instances these organizations gained a more balanced and *integrated view* of their business at "3rd Base." And making these amazing discoveries and translating them into focused strategies enabled them to align their organization to get the right things done.

"3rd base" is where internal and external analyses come together and we can determine how to become *someone else's worst nightmare*. It is here that that we can assess if we are truly delivering what our customers want. It is here that we are able to visualize where we are vulnerable to competition and where we are strong and have an opportunity to dominate.

There are various ways that we can conduct competitive gap analysis. In the following pages we will review a methodology that has been proven to work and produced positive results.

We will convert the three bubbles on the left side of the Strategic Scan® into a value-added "Assembly Line."

The "Assembly Line" is comprised of 14 attributes to evaluate and compare the needs of our customers vs. our own strengths and weaknesses and vs. the strengths and weaknesses of our competitors *(Figure 17 – Assembly Line )*.

*Figure 17 –* ***Assembly Line®***

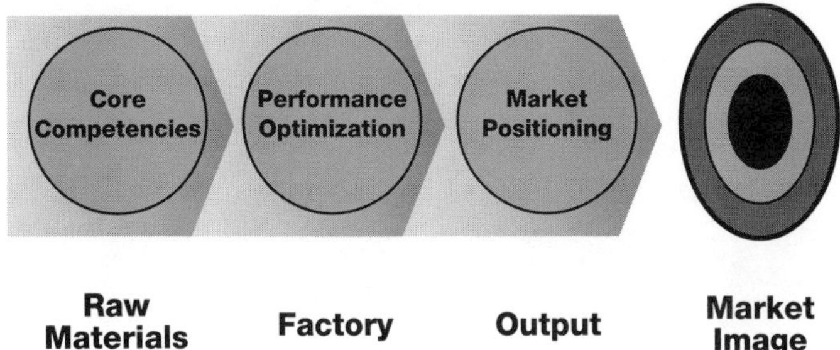


The "Assembly Line" is comprised of three components:

***Core Competencies*** or "Raw Materials" are the things that we need to do extremely well. They form the basis for sustainable competitive differentiation.

***Performance Optimization*** or the "Factory" is how we will measure and manage our resources to achieve exceptional performance.

***Market Positioning*** or the "Output" is how we will consistently create value for our customers.

*Figure 18 –* ***Assembly Line***

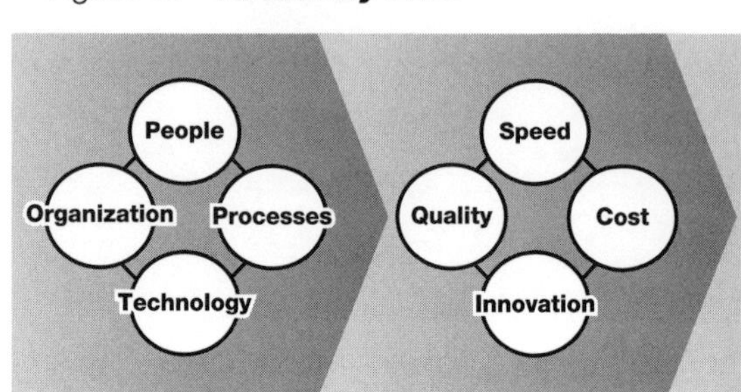


**Raw Materials** **Factory**

Let's now see the "Assembly Line" in more detail to understand how it can be converted into an effective, 14-attribute competitive assessment tool *(Figure 18 – Assembly Line)*.

"***Raw Materials***" – The things we need to do extremely well:

- ***People*** – Critical skills, experience, and know-how,
- ***Organization*** – Organizational relationships across our value chain and among our various departments and staff,
- ***Processes*** – Those that are critical to our success, e.g. Order processing, complaint handling, new product development, or purchasing, and
- ***Technology*** – Proprietary and or uniquely applied technologies

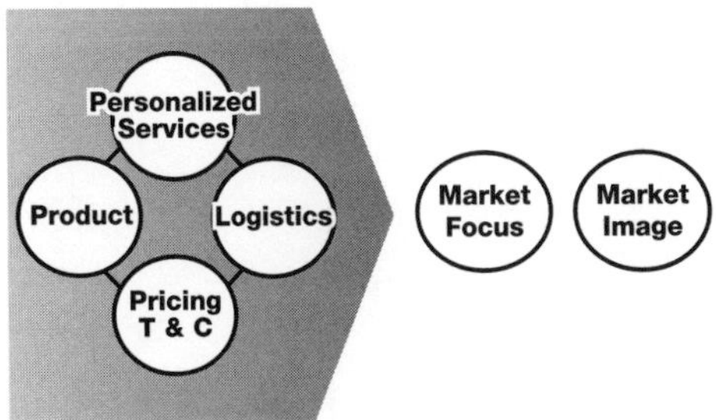


**Output** **Market Image**

The "***Factory***" – How we will optimize our "raw materials":

- ***Speed*** – Our sense of urgency. Our ability to anticipate and quickly address issues and opportunities,
- ***Quality*** – Our ability to do things right the first time, every time,
- ***Cost Reductions*** – Our ability to run an efficient and low cost operation, and
- ***Innovation*** – Our ability to deliver first-of-a-kind products and services as well as new creative ways of conducting business.

"***Output***" – The four mechanisms we have to create value for our customers (Please refer to '2nd base" in Chapter 4):

- Personalized services,
- Product/service attributes,
- Logistical or delivery performance, and
- Pricing and terms.

*Figure 19* – ***Self Assessment***

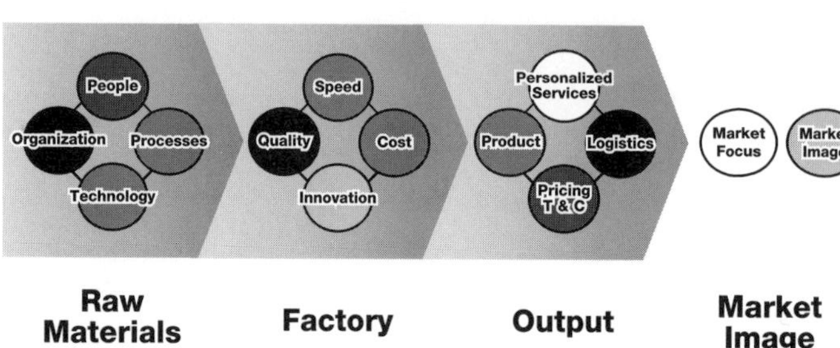


A well-tuned "Assembly Line" will deliver superior value to our targeted markets. By *focusing* our energies and resources on markets that we choose to dominate, we will establish a positive *market image* and achieve superior results.

We can now assess our effectiveness and that of our competitors by coding the bubbles utilizing a five-shade spectrum: White bubbles for exceptional performance, a light shade of gray for very good performance and so on until we get to the black bubbles for poor performance *(Figure 19 – Self Assessment)*.

This is a very important exercise and we should not rely on internal information alone. Sometimes we are too hard on ourselves. Other times we suffer from a false sense of security and believe that we are unbeatable.

Where else can get the information? We can ask our customers, our employees, ex-employees of our competitors, attend business shows, or hire experts in our field. Ultimately, the scores are subjective, but once we have information that we can trust, we will be able to visualize the real issues and the opportunities.

Imagine that the example above depicts our organization. We enjoy a very good market image, perhaps because we are delivering exceptional personalized services and we are extremely focused on certain markets (see right side of the model). However, our "Raw Materials" and our "Factory" are not in good shape (left side). Over time, the darkest grays and blacks will migrate to the right and cover the entire "Assembly Line." Our organization is in trouble and does not have a sustainable advantage. This chart is a call to action for us to rebuild ourselves from the inside out.

On the other hand, if our organization possessed strong "Raw Materials" and a strong "Factory," we would be positioned to be a dominant player.

The model can be used to evaluate our entire organization or any portion of our organization. Also, it can be used to evaluate our *most feared competitors*. Finally, we can use it to assess where *our targeted customers* look for exceptional performance from their suppliers (white), and where they place less importance.

Let's see now how we can use the model to conduct our gap analysis.

Figure 20 – **Customer Gap Analysis**

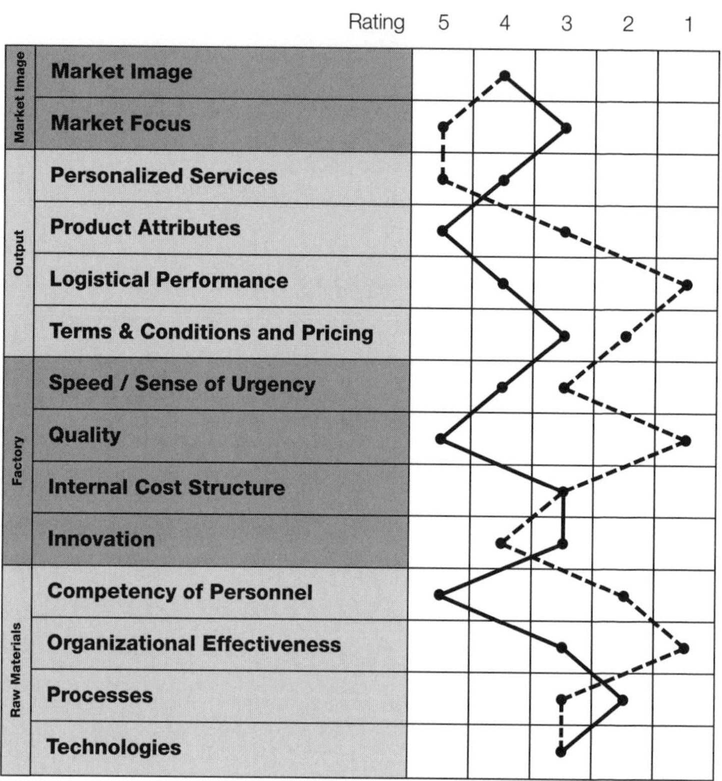


By simply rearranging how information is displayed, *(Figure 20 – Customer Gap Analysis)* we can compare our customers' priorities with our own strengths and weaknesses

The "Assembly Line" that appeared horizontally in *Figure 18 – Assembly Line*, now appears along a vertical axis. The example that I showed you in *Figure 19 – Self Assessment* now appears as a dashed zigzag line where a 5 is exceptional and a 1 is poor or non-competitive.

Assume for one moment that the dashed zigzag line represents our strengths and weaknesses, and the solid zigzag represents our customers' priorities. That is, what they told us at "2nd base."

If it were a true situation, it should give us reasons to worry, and motivation to act. Notice the importance that our customers place on product and logistical performance compared to our own mediocre or unsatisfactory performance. Observe also, how critical it is for our customers that we deliver top quality and that we have highly competent personnel.

When doing this analysis, assume always that customers are continually doing this type of comparison. Therefore, remember:

---

**If we don't prioritize on what's important for our customers, sooner or later they will prioritize us off of their list.**

---

Now let's compare our own strengths and weaknesses against our competitors' strengths and weaknesses.

*Figure 21* – ***Competitor Gap Analysis***

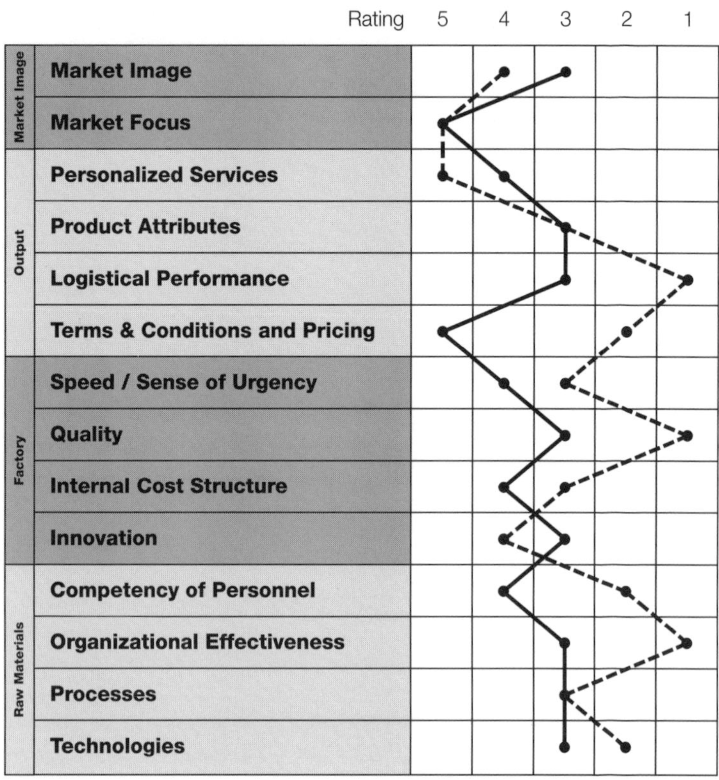


The dashed zigzag line *(Figure 21 – Competitor Gap Analysis)*, as before, represents our strengths and weaknesses. The solid zigzag line now represents the strengths and weaknesses of our competitor. If this were a true situation, it should give us additional reasons to worry and to take action. Notice how our competitor is positioned to deliver value to our customers through personalized services, product attributes, logistics, and pricing and terms. Observe also, that our competitor has relatively strong "Raw Materials" and an effective "Factory" (bottom half of the model). If our competitor were analyzing this chart, it could choose to strengthen its product attributes and deal us a mortal blow.

The "Assembly Line" model can help us turn the tables on our competitors. But we must be sure that our executive team is fully aware of the implications revealed in this analysis. They must *understand* the choices before them and be prepared to take action. Otherwise, we risk allowing our competitors to become our *own worst nightmare*.

*When* in doubt remember this simple rule:

---

**If it is good for our customers and for us, and it is bad for our competitors, it is probably the right thing to do.**

---

*Figure 22 – **Integrated View***

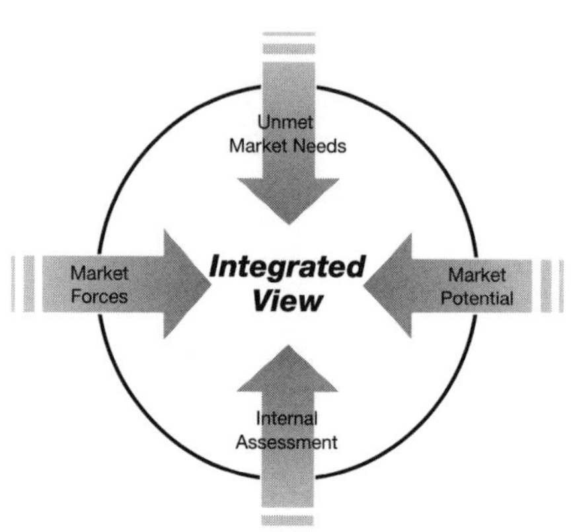


This chapter concludes our discussions on simple but powerful "thinking models" that can help us develop an *integrated view* of our environment in order to *discover our best opportunities (Figure 22 – Integrated View)*.

However, if we are to realize the full potential of this System, we must engage our entire leadership team to prioritize:

- *How* to become a dominant player across our critical path for profit at "1st base,"
- *How* to build partnership relationships and become our customers #1 choice at "2nd base," and
- *How* to become our competitors' worst nightmare at "3rd Base."

Only then will we have an executive team that has the necessary *depth of understanding* to make the right choices, and is *committed* to get the right things done.

Getting the right things done is what "Home Plate" and the following chapters are all about.

# 6

## ***Coming "Home"***

Coming "Home" is about determining where we must excel to *unleash our best opportunities (Figure 23 – Strategic Scan®; Figure 24 – Running the Bases)*. It requires that our leadership team fully *understands* our environment, and has the *courage* and *commitment* to get it done.

As you read the following chapters, remember the good window cleaners discussed at the beginning of this book. They focus on the corners making sure they are cleaned perfectly. Then, they complete the rest of the window with minimal effort.

Our job as executives is to find the "corners," those few things in our organization where our entire team must be *aligned* to do the right things extremely well.

But if our executives don't have a *shared* and *integrated view* of our internal and external environments, they may not be prepared to make the tough choices nor committed to take appropriate action. The danger, of course, is that as an organization we revert to past experiences and personal preferences and continue doing what we have been doing all along.

Figure 23 – ***Strategic Scan***®

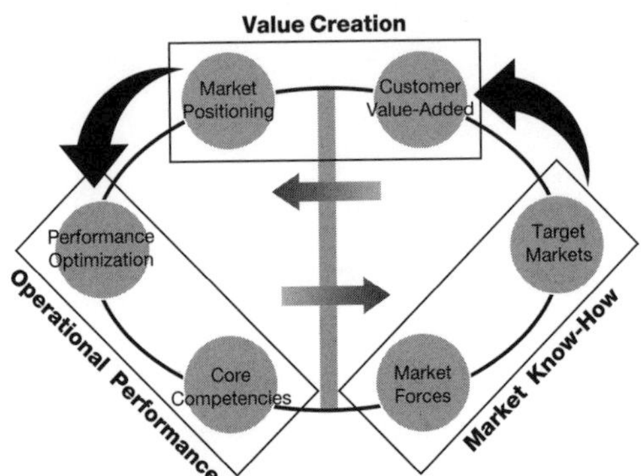


Figure 24 – ***Running the Bases***

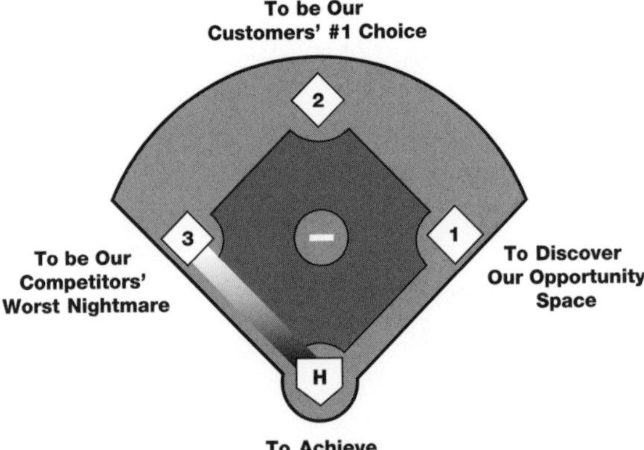

Earlier we discussed the importance of establishing stretch goals to bring ourselves to that thin line between what is possible and what is impossible. We discussed why we needed to step out of our comfort zone from time to time and discover creative ideas to achieve what may at first appear "impossible."

As we complete our environmental analysis, we will uncover challenges and opportunities that we must address to meet or exceed our stretch goals. Typically we come up with 70 to 100 good ideas that then become raw material from which to choose and *unleash our best opportunities*.

Our first challenge will be to transform these good ideas into a clearly articulated vision statement and a set of prioritized strategies, tactics and action plans. This will enable us to effectively communicate our plan inside and outside our organization.

Our stretch goals will now play another important role. They will act like a "stake in the ground" to help us integrate our vision, strategies, tactics and action plans into a cohesive strategic plan.

To illustrate how this works, imagine that our stretch goal is to double revenues and profits in the next three years. If asked *why* we are pursuing this goal, we may say: "We want to be recognized as the undisputed leader in our chosen niche." With this answer we have established a greater purpose for our quest (our vision) and linked it to our stretch goal.

*Figure 25 –* ***Strategic Ladder®***

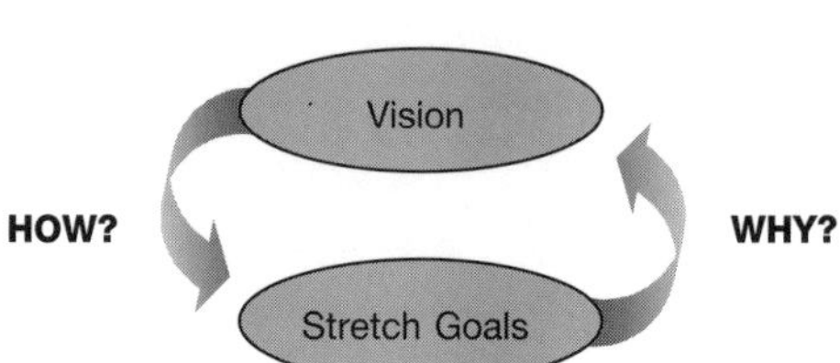


The Strategic Ladder® *(Figure 25 – Strategic Ladder®)* reinforces the concept that our "unique universe" is comprised of consistent cause-and-effect dynamics.

Just as there is a "how" and "why" relationship between our stretch goals and our vision, there is a "how" and "why" relationship among our stretch goals, strategies, tactics and action plans *(Figure 26 – Strategic Ladder®)*.

When we complete our plan, we need to establish tight linkages among the various elements of our plan. Strategies become longer-term "projects" that can last 2-3 years. Tactics (which support our strategies) become medium term "projects" that typically last 6-12 months. Action Plans (which support our Tactics) become short-term "projects" that last 30-60-90 days. All of them are linked by the questions, "how?" and "why?"

*Figure 26* – ***Strategic Ladder®***

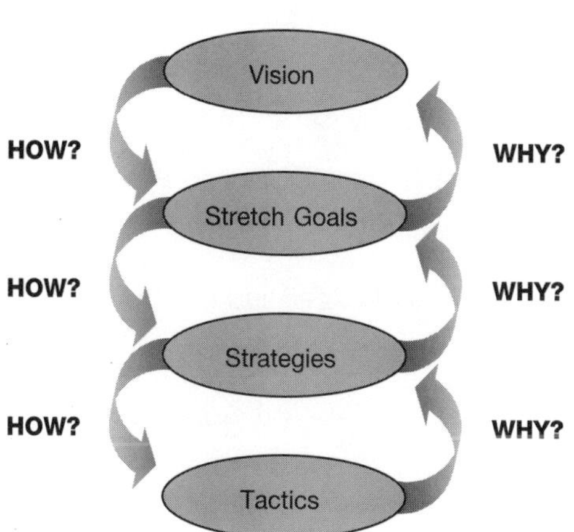


A person responsible for a given tactic, for example, needs to know what is the expected outcome (the "why") of his or her actions. In this case, the strategy provides the answer.

Going in the opposite direction, the owner of a particular strategy needs to execute a set of tactics (the "how") in order to successfully implement his or her strategy.

### *Making a Difference*

As we learned on "2nd Base," we can create value for someone every time we help them either increase revenues, reduce costs and/or feel good.

Each strategy and tactic should create value *for our customers* and *for us*. This will keep everyone focused outwardly toward the customer while making the necessary improvements internally.

For example, if our *strategy* is to "build sustainable partnerships with key players across our value chain," we can strengthen and clarify our intent to create value as follows:

The intent of our strategy is:

- To make it easier for our customers to do business with us (value created for our customers), and
- To get our products specified by end users (value created for us)

If our tactic is to "implement a continuous improvement program," we can strengthen and clarify our intent to create value as follows:

The intent of our tactic is:

- To enhance our ability to deliver on our promises first time every time (value created for our customers), and
- To minimize costs across the entire value chain (value created for us)

Value-added intent statements make the expected outcome very clear to the person responsible for a particular strategy or tactic. They also provide us the basis for establishing our performance measurements. (Please see Chapter 7)

### *What Our Customers Really Want*

To create value we need to be brutally honest with ourselves. Prioritizing on things that our customers are willing to pay for is key. Prioritizing 'til it hurts means discontinuing pet projects and products that we want to work on but our customers don't want or need. This is as hard for a CEO as it is for anyone else.

*Figure 27* – **Strategic Ladder®**

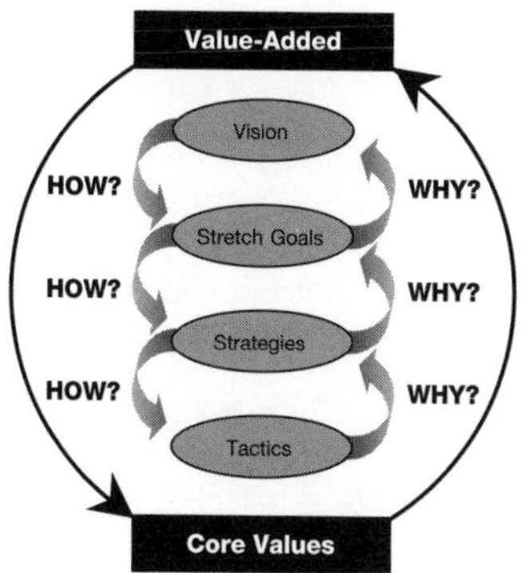


---

**Our customers care little about our vision, goals and strategy statements. They care an awful lot about the *value* we create for them and about our *core values* or the behaviors our organization exemplifies.**

---

These two elements are like an aura that we project onto our customers each and every time we interface with them. Together they form the basis of our *market image (Figure 27 – Strategic Ladder®)*.

To illustrate how this works, I will use as an example two athletes who want to win the Tennis Grand Slam. One wants to be recognized as the best tennis player in the world (*his vision*) and is committed to delivering top performance every time he's on the court (*his value added*). "Integrity," "Perseverance," and "Respect for others" are his *core values*.

The other wants to be the richest athlete in the world (*his vision*) and is committed to entertaining crowds on and off the court (*his value added*). "Personal self image," "Lots of Money," and "Having control over any situation" are his *core values*.

I am sure we can all think of athletes who fall into each of these categories. We may have found ourselves watching these types of athletes perform either because they provided us exhilarating performance or entertainment (their value added) or because we admired or were amused by their behavior (reflection of their core values). I doubt that we were attracted to them because of their vision, strategies, tactics and action plans.

When we assemble our strategic plans, we need to pay special attention to these two elements. Our customers will make their choices between our competitors and us based on the value that we create for them, and how our organization behaves toward them and toward the marketplace at large. This cause-and-effect dynamic is predictable.

### *Completing the Model*

To reinforce how the Strategic Ladder® works, let's continue the tennis player analogy. Assuming they both want to win the Grand Slam, here's how they would arrive at their Strategies and their Tactics.

By asking *how* they can achieve their goal, they will come up with a list of potential Strategies (long term "projects"). For example: "Implement a continuous physical fitness improvement program."

*Figure 28* – ***Strategic Ladder®***

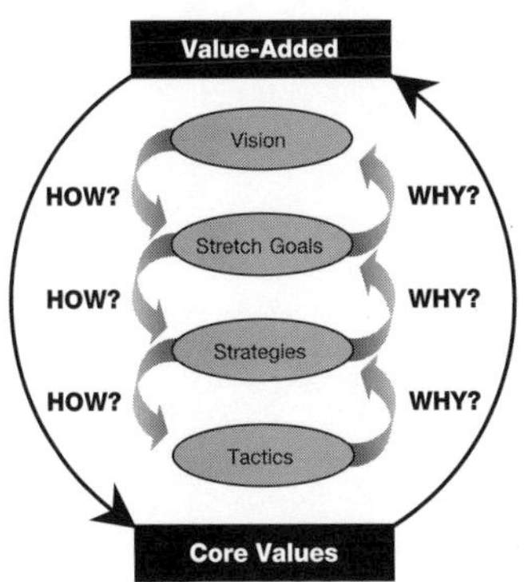


Then, by asking "how" they can achieve their Strategies, they would come up with a list of potential Tactics (shorter-term projects). For example: "Engage a world renowned trainer and coach."

Finally, by asking, "how" they can achieve their Tactics, they would come up with a list of day-to-day activities that need to be implemented. For example: "Run 6 miles each day."

If they come up, from time to time, with new opportunities or challenges to work on, all they need to ask is "why" and they would know if these fit within their strategic plan or not. If they don't fit, then they probably shouldn't do them.

That's how they would continually prioritize 'til it hurts and stay focused on excelling on things that really matter *(Figure 28 – Strategic Ladder®)*.

Consider the number of times that we are presented with opportunities, distractions and other things to worry about that don't fit within our strategic plan. Imagine the power of having this model clearly in our mind, knowing without a doubt when we need to say, "YES" and when we must say "NO"!

# 7

# *Aligning Our Operation*

## *Performance Measures*

---

**Performance measurements comprise perhaps the most powerful force available to us to achieve complete alignment across our operation.**

---

Here's why:

From the time we were able to think and talk, we started measuring everything that mattered to us. Measurements have driven our behavior and to a great extent they have made us who we are.

Measurements are a powerful force that if properly applied, can energize an organization to accomplish incredible feats. Think about when you were very young. What did you measure? Wasn't it those things that were really important to you?

Did you count number of toys you received? How many times your mom and dad told you they loved you? How many friends you had?

As you grew older and became a teenager, what did you measure? Was it the number of sports trophies you received? Was it your grades in school? Was it how well you were accepted by your peers?

Think about how you, without thinking, turned your priorities into personal performance measures and how these, in turn, became a powerful force which drove (and still drives) your behavior.

Imagine the positive force that we can unleash if we measure and reward everyone in our organization on doing what's right for our customers.

In the early 1980's, I witnessed that force while visiting with a Honda executive in Tokyo. He explained that his company had established one primary performance metric: To reduce the time required to process an order and deliver an automobile from Japan to a U.S. customer from 28 days to 14 days. They needed to make dramatic improvements in speed of delivery while maintaining their high quality standards and lowering their costs. This was their key strategy for becoming a preferred supplier to the US consumer.

At the time of my visit, they had rallied everyone, including their US automobile agencies, suppliers, production managers, administrative and IT personnel around specific measures to achieve their primary objective. As a result, they were soon able to achieve their 14-day goal.

Not realizing that I was about to be taught a lesson, I asked the manager, "what will you do when your Managing Director tells you that 14 days is not good enough, and that you must now deliver the automobile in 8 days?" He smiled and said: "We will eliminate the Pacific Ocean." (It was at about this time that Honda was initiating automobile manufacturing operations at its Marysville, Ohio plant.)

The results are now history. The Honda Accord became a top-selling automobile in the US and has remained so for the past 20 years.

By getting everyone focused on just a few critical measures we can unleash a continuous improvement process to deliver exceptional performance to our customers and for our company. It is important; however, to emphasize that Honda did not focus on speed alone. They made speed the *primary driver* while maintaining excellent quality and competitive costs.

The lessons learned are these:

- Measurements, properly applied, can help us to *unleash our best opportunities*. If there are processes that need to be fixed, they will be fixed. If there are processes that need to be created, they will be created. If there are skills that need to be developed, they will be developed.
- If Honda had measured speed alone, it is likely their quality would have suffered, their inventories would have reached unreasonable levels, and their costs would have risen as a result. Therefore, in selecting your few critical measures, always remember to implement counter measures to assure balanced performance across your organization.

---

**Performance measurements can cause our organization to focus on what's truly important, create a habit of doing things better all the time, and motivate employees to create significant value for our customers.**

---

Ultimately they can lead to a sustainable competitive advantage.

However, they can also cause problems if not implemented in a way that assures balanced performance across the organization.

Therefore, I offer these six guidelines for implementing a performance measurement program:

1 – Align your measurements with your strategic priorities. Remember that we become what we measure.

2 – Select counter measures to produce balanced performance. For example: Measure speed of delivery in combination with quality and cost of delivery. Or measure manufacturing velocity in combination with incoming quality, outgoing quality and cost.

3 – Start with a few metrics, and then add new ones as you gain experience and become comfortable with the process. Make sure your organization is assimilating and learning to operate within a performance driven environment.

4 – Establish a simple, low maintenance tracking and reporting system. Don't add another bureaucratic process to your operation.

5 – Celebrate the rate of improvement, not your latest results. It is dangerous to turn the process into a punitive system. Always remember that continuous improvement is the goal.

6 – Fix the root cause, not the symptom. Your objective is to eliminate problems permanently.

Figure 29 – **Operational Alignment**

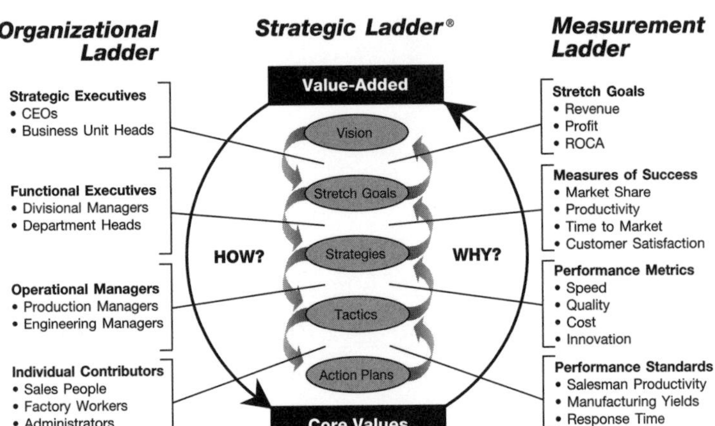


### ***Aligning Your Organization***

The three Ladders *(Figure 29 – Operational Alignment)* provide an added dimension for aligning our organization with our strategic plan. Notice the relationship as we move horizontally across the three Ladders. For example, as we move from left to right:

- Strategic executives (at the top) are challenged with the longer-term vision and financial success of the company.
- Individual contributors (at the bottom) are responsible for shorter-term action plans and for their individual performance.

*Figure 30 –* ***Operational Alignment***

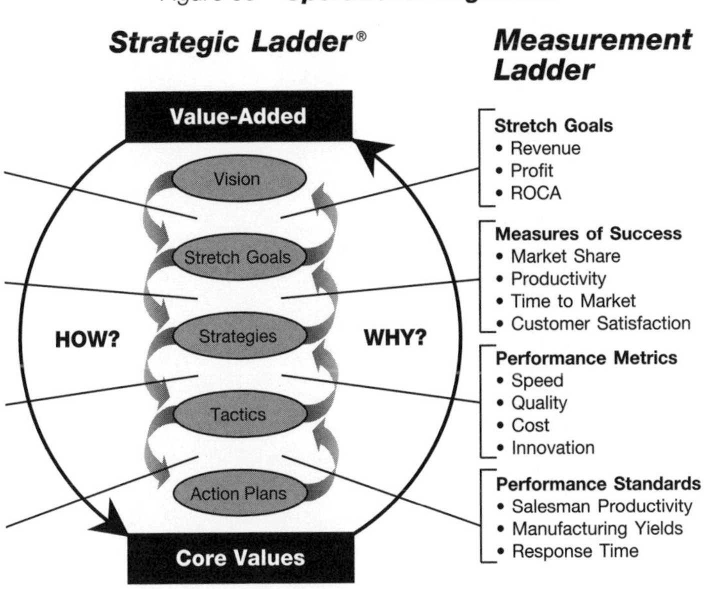


### *The Measurement Ladder (On the Right)*

Note the cause-and-effect dynamics (the "how" and "why" linkages) as we move from the bottom to the top of the Measurement Ladder *(Figure 30 – Operational Alignment)*. The lower portion of the Ladder deals with short-term performance measures (or *leading indicators*) that are prerequisites to achieving the higher-level goals. The upper portion of the Measurement Ladder deals with longer term financial outcomes such as Revenue, Profits and Return on Capital Assets (or *trailing indicators*) that are a reflection of how well work was done in the past.

*Figure 31 –* ***Operational Alignment***

### *The Organizational Ladder (On the Left)*

The Organizational Ladder *(Figure 30 – Operational Alignment)* shows how the cause-and-effect dynamics (the "how" and the" why" linkages) still apply. It shows how people in our organization will relate to each other.

---

**Getting everyone focused on how they can all contribute to maximizing results is the quickest and most effective way to get them aligned around a common purpose.**

---

Chances are, that initially only our leadership team will be privy to our plans. Soon after, we need to communicate the plan and align everyone in our organization to implement the plan.

It is critically important that everyone understand, from his or her perspective, where we are taking the organization.

We need to use language that everyone understands. Shop floor workers, for example, may not tune in when we talk to them about maximizing profit potential and achieving a sustainable competitive advantage. However, they will be energized by understanding the general direction of our organization, our core values, how each of them can contribute to create value for our company and for our customers, and how they will benefit as individuals and as a team.

Remember the Honda example at the beginning of this chapter. Getting their automobile agencies, suppliers, production managers, administrative and IT personnel all pulling in the same direction required that each group know, in terms relevant to them, what they needed to do and why they needed to do it.

# 8

## Creating Our Mission Statement

Mission statements, which are not written with the customer in mind, run the risk of creating little value in the long run.

Too often, mission statements (or statements of purpose) describe *how* an organization has decided to position itself in the marketplace, not to communicate the resulting benefits the organization creates for its customers. When composing our mission statement we need to ask ourselves, "why should our customers want to do business with us and no one else?"

Perhaps a few examples will illustrate my point:

Imagine we own a company that manufactures drills. We have two mission statements to pick from: One describes the high quality, precision and durability of our drills. The other, by contrast, is very simple: "We help our customers make perfect holes every time."

I propose using the latter for several reasons: First it is a unifying concept to keep our organization focused on creating value for the customer. Second, it communicates our value-added in a language the customer understands and appreciates.

Third, it encourages everyone in our organization to continually investigate and pursue new and innovative ways to "make perfect holes every time." And fourth, it defines and communicates our identifiable difference in the marketplace.

Following are several good examples of actual mission statements:

***Jason International***

"We make bathing enjoyable"

***Boys Scouts of America:***

"Prepare young people to make ethical choices over their lifetime and to achieve their full potential"

***Microsoft:***

"To enable people and businesses throughout the world to realize their full potential"

***Ursuline College's Statement of Purpose:***

"We help students succeed in life"

To know that we have an effective mission statement, I use what I call the "cocktail test." Imagine that we are a cocktail party (or at business conference) and someone asks us what our company does. Consider the alternatives:

***Example:***

"Our company prides itself in making the best drills in the industry"

vs.

"We help our customers make perfect holes every time"

***Jason International:***

"We design and manufacture a full line of luxury baths"

vs.

"We make bathing enjoyable"

***DHD Healthcare:***

"We commercialize innovative breathing equipment"

vs.

"Our innovative products help people breathe easier"

***Dialight:***

"We design and commercialize solutions utilizing LEDs"

vs.

"We make LEDs usable™"

---

**When we communicate the outcome of what we do, and the value that it creates, our audience will become intrigued and want to know more about us.**

---

Value-added outcome statements create wonderful opportunities to get the attention of people outside and inside our organization. It peaks their interest to want to know how we make it happen.

To get started, go back to the Voice of the Customer on "2nd base" (Chapter 4) and see what your customers are yearning for from their *partner*. Remember they always want someone that can help them "grow revenues," "reduce costs" and/or "feel good." Search and you too will find the perfect way to communicate how you create (or plan to create) unique value for your customers.

# 9

## *Getting Started*

In this book we have reviewed ways to make our "unique universe" seem logical and approachable, and described a roadmap for discovering our "Acres of Diamonds."

Now you may ask: "How do we get started?"

Imagine that you are about to undertake a journey of discovery. A well thought out journey that will uncover new and realistic possibilities for growth. The process itself is not rocket science, but it will require, more than anything else, your *total commitment* and that of your leadership team.

Here's what you must make sure happens at the outset:

***First***, confirm in your own mind that this is a journey you really want to make. One that will produce value for your customers and for you. One to which you will enthusiastically provide your personal leadership.

If your objective is simply to fulfill an annual corporate ritual, stop. You will be disappointed with the results you achieve. Chances are that your plan will end up, as many others have, in a filing cabinet.

Figure 32 – **Integrated View**

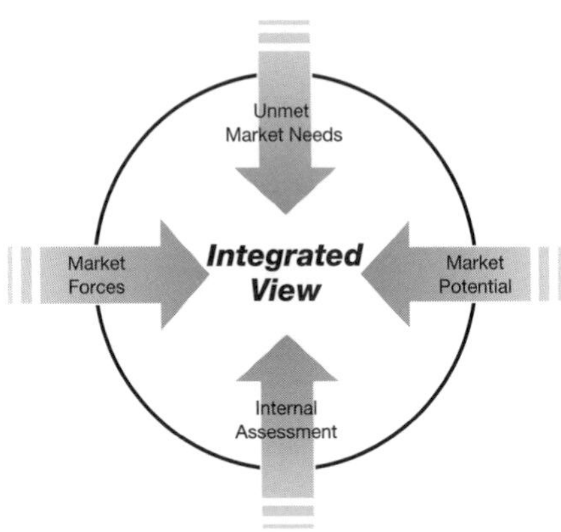


***Second***, commit the resources to build a solid foundation based on an *integrated view* of your "unique universe." That's how you will keep your plan from being swept away like a sand castle with the rising tides.

I'm sure you have heard the expression "garbage in - garbage out." So gather the best information you can about your targeted markets, your customers' unmet needs, and the major forces surrounding them. Then, conduct a critical analysis of your own organization to understand the strengths you can leverage and the areas where you are vulnerable *(Figure 32 – Integrated View)*.

***Third***, Organize your journey:

> ***Destination*** – establish aggressive *targets*, or stretch goals, that will point you toward a worthwhile and challenging destination.
>
> ***Roadmap*** – select a process that has been tested and has delivered positive results to others.

*Figure 33 –* ***Discovery Life Cycle©***

***Schedule*** – commit to a *time line* with milestones to gauge your progress,

***Guide*** – engage an experienced *coach* or *facilitator* with the business acumen, creative mind, and a bias for helping you succeed, and

***Travel Companions*** - select the *participants* who will form your planning and execution team. Actively engage them in the process from start to finish to raise their level of *understanding* and *commitment*.

As you *proceed* on your journey *(Figure 33 – Discovery Life Cycle©)* make sure that you:

- *Center your thinking on the customer and the marketplace,*
- *Explore all possibilities,*
- *Prioritize 'til it hurts, and*
- *Commit to (and implement) a follow-up process.*

*Figure 34 –* ***Discovery Life Cycle***©

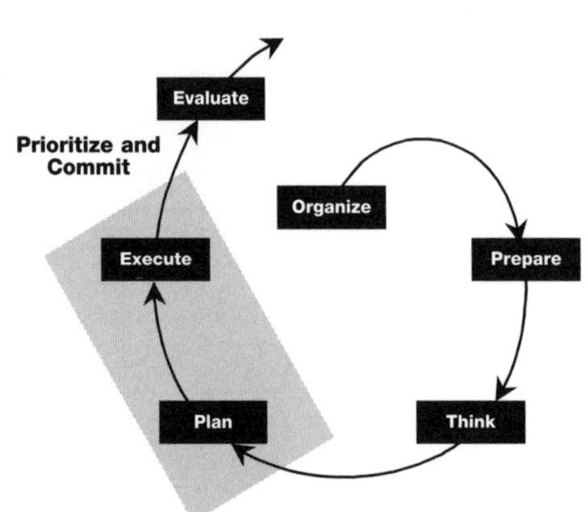


### ***Building a Credible Plan***

If you are like most people, you will be impatient and want to start acting on your plan *(Figure 34 – Discovery Life Cycle©)*. The success of your plan will depend on its effective execution. However, the danger in acting prematurely is that your plan may be out of context with the realities of your external environment, and out of range for your current capabilities. Your customers are reacting to changes in their industry and to new demands from their own customers. Their needs and expectations are continually changing as new technological breakthroughs take place, and your competitors present them with new and creative solutions to their problems.

The strategies that made sense yesterday may not make sense today. Therefore, follow the process. Take the time to *organize*, *prepare* and *think* before making your final choices.

You will be surprised at how quickly you can develop your winning plan.

### *Prepare and Think*

Once you get yourself organized for your journey, "step out of the box" and discover the possibilities. Remember that you must eventually refocus and "step back into a box" with a focused plan for action which is *relevant*, *credible*, *challenging* and *achievable*.

The purpose of the *preparation* phase is to thoroughly *understand* your internal and external environments and develop an *integrated view* of your "unique universe." (Please refer to Chapters 1 through 5)

---

**Without credible, integrated and up-to-date information you risk building a plan that is based purely on past experience and emotion.**

---

*Figure 35 –* ***Discovery Life Cycle©***

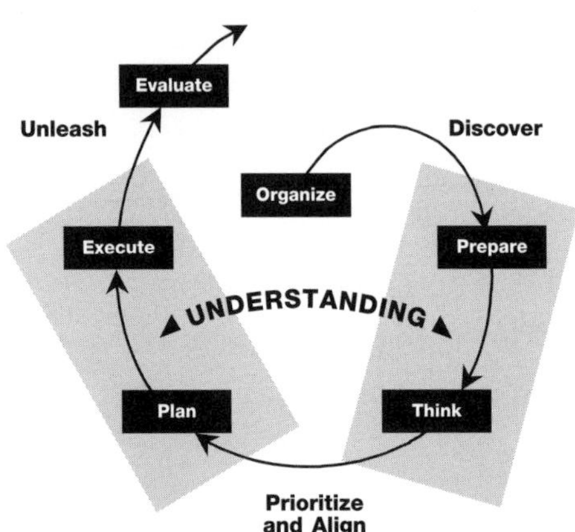


### ***Plan***

As you "step out" and again as you "step back" you need to keep your planning team *involved*. This is all part of the *discovery* process *(Figure 35 – Discovery Life Cycle©)*. Your planning team must *experience* and *learn* from the journey. Otherwise, it will not have the level of *understanding* of the total business to effectively help you *prioritize*, and make the tough choices and *unleash your best opportunities*.

The step-by-step journey that you took to develop an *integrated view* of your "unique universe," will now serve you well to assess and evaluate your strategies and tactics. You can be confident that your plan will lead to a sustainable competitive advantage if you can demonstrate that it:

**1st Base**

- Targets markets that offer you the greatest potential for profitable growth,

**2nd Base**

- Anticipates major opportunities and challenges in your marketplace,
- Creates unique value for your customers,

**3rd Base**

- Establishes a clear identifiable difference,

**Home Plate**

- Optimizes your performance across your value chain,
- Builds competencies for long-term advantage,
- Raises barriers to competition, and has the potential to change the rules of play in your marketplace.

Figure 36 – **Discovery Life Cycle©**

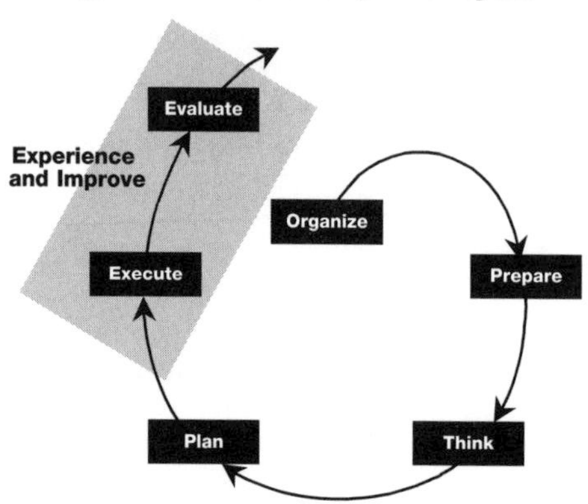


### ***Execute and Evaluate***

The best possible plans do not guarantee success. In fact, they are merely the beginning. Don't stop! Continue your journey. Evaluate your performance, learn from your successes and your failures, improve your plan and continue to execute *(Figure 36 – Discovery Life Cycle©)*.

All sports teams do this. Think about it. Have you ever attended a children's sports game where a half a dozen parents weren't videotaping the event? Professional sports teams do the same thing; they review their videotapes from last Saturday's games, pinpoint where they need to improve and put plans in place to win next Saturday's game. Do you do this? If not, how do you expect to win "next Saturday's game"?

Doing something concrete within thirty days of completing your plan is absolutely necessary. It's very much like reaching critical speed on the runway so that your airplane can gain flight. Not taking those first few steps will cause inertia to set in and increase the risk that current business pressures will overtake your best intentions… your plan will likely end up in a filing cabinet.

A quarterly maintenance process supported with a performance improvement program will keep your "airplane" in flight. It will enable you to keep your organization aligned. It will instill the concept of continuous improvement into your corporate culture. It will keep you on course.

# 10

## *Predictable Cause-and-Effect Dynamics (A Summary)*

Throughout this book I have shared predictable dynamics that have become guideposts in my life. They have helped me stay on track and make good decisions when faced with adversity. In this final chapter, I summarize them for you:

### *On Prioritization*

- If we don't prioritize on what's important for our customers, sooner or later they will prioritize us off of their list.
- Unless we prioritize, we may work very hard, but never excel at anything.
- When we do a few things extremely well, we cause many other things to improve.
- If we don't make the tough choices, we leave to chance where it is that we will excel, and in the end rarely achieve major success.

### *On Discovering the Possibilities*

- There is always new news. If unfolding events catch us by surprise, we are likely to miss opportunities and suffer the consequences.
- Without credible and up-to-date information, we will build plans that are based purely on past experience and emotion.
- Sometimes the best ideas are hidden. When searching for major opportunities or facing critical situations, we need to take the time to uncover every possibility before coming up with our final short list.

### *On Value Creation*

- When we communicate the outcome of what we do, and the value that it creates, our audience will become intrigued and want to know more about us.
- Our customers care little about our vision, goals and strategy statements. They care an awful lot about the value we create for them and about our core values. Together they form the basis for our market image.
- Sustained revenue and profit growth is our customers' way of telling us that we have exceeded their expectations and that they appreciate what we do for them.

### ***On Business Relationships***

- *Partners* who work together to grow revenues (make money), lower costs (save money), and enjoy their relationship (feel good)… will stay together.
- *Suppliers* remain suppliers by performing or excelling along four dimensions: personalized services, product and service attributes, delivery performance, and terms & conditions (including price).
- "Connecting the dots" between what our customers tell us they need to achieve *their success* (as partners), and what we need to do to help them achieve *their success* (as their supplier), is crucial to aligning our organization to achieve *our own success*.

### ***On Alignment***

- Organizational misalignment always begins with a change in the marketplace that went unnoticed by us.
- Getting everyone focused on how they can all contribute to maximizing results is the quickest and most effective way to get them aligned around a common purpose.
- When we align our organization, and channel our resources to accomplish a common purpose, everyone will feel a sense of pride and satisfaction, and get the right things done.

### ***Final Guidepost***

- If it is good for our customers and us, and it is bad for our competitors, it is probably the right thing to do.

# *Cause-and-Effect "Thinking Models"*

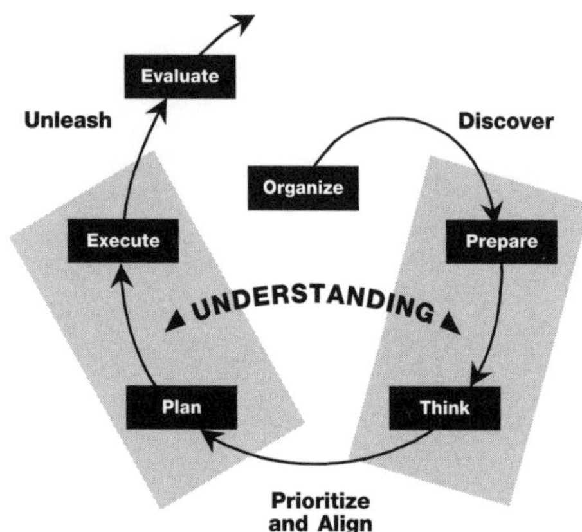
Discovery Life Cycle©
Evaluate
Unleash
Discover
Organize
Execute
Prepare
UNDERSTANDING
Plan
Think
Prioritize and Align

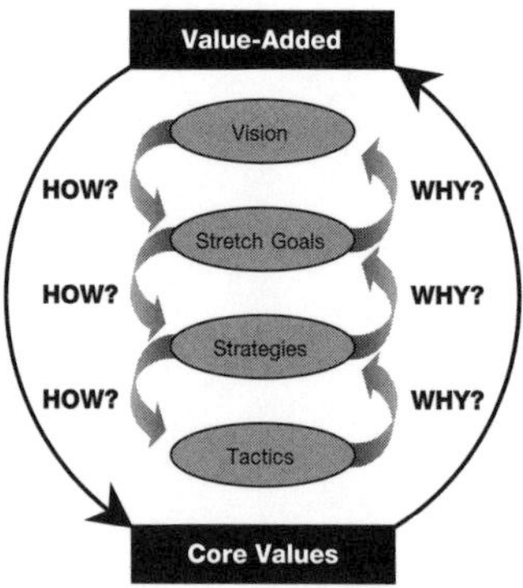
Strategic Ladder®
Value-Added
Vision
HOW?
WHY?
Stretch Goals
HOW?
WHY?
Strategies
HOW?
WHY?
Tactics
Core Values

## Strategic Scan®

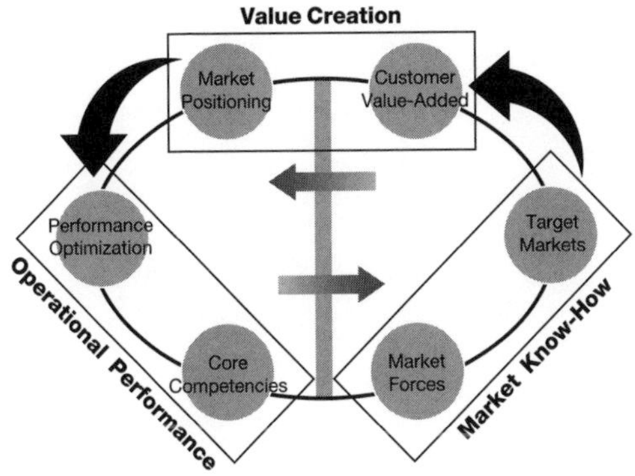


## Strategic Scan®

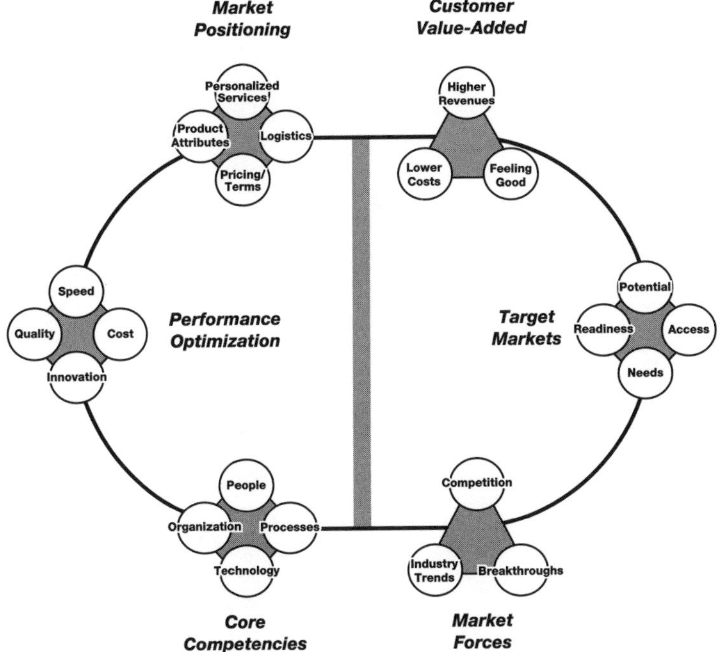

### *About the Author and the System:*

Rodolfo Salas is founder and president of RSR International. Since 1992 he has perfected the Prioritize 'til It Hurts System while assisting thousands of executives worldwide.

Mr. Salas is a graduate of Yale University and a former executive with IBM and Rockwell Automation. Throughout his 30-year business career he was repeatedly recognized for his leadership, creativity and superior results in difficult situations.

My book may very well raise more questions than it answers. If such is the case, please do not hesitate to call me. You may also contact and/or learn more about our Team and about the System by visiting our Web Page: www.PrioritizeTillItHurts.com

Rody Salas

Rodolfo Salas
P.O. Box 491
Chagrin Falls, Ohio, U.S.A 44022
Telephone: 440 / 247-5201